RESOLVING

Biblical Answers

everyday

for a Common Problem

CONFLICT

HENDRICKSON
PUBLISHERS

www.hendrickson.com
www.Peacemaker.net

PEACEMAKER®
MINISTRIES

Peacemaker® Ministries

Peacemaker Ministries is a 501(c)(3) non-profit organization that was founded in 1982 to equip
and assist Christians and their churches to respond to conflict biblically.

Version 3.1

Hendrickson Publishers Marketing, LLC
P. O. Box 3473
Peabody, Massachusetts 01961-3473
www.hendrickson.com

ISBN 978-1-68307-099-3

This publication is designed to provide general information on biblical conflict resolution within
churches. It is not intended to provide legal or other professional advice. If legal counsel or other
expert assistance is required, the services of a competent professional should be sought.

Scripture quotations taken from The Holy Bible, English Standard Version® (ESV®) Copyright ©
2001 by Crossway, a publishing ministry of Good News Publishers.
All rights reserved. ESV Text Edition: 2011

Cover images: tree © depositphotos/carloscastilla; sky © depositphotos/lunamarina

Cover Design by RJS Design

Interior design and production by Scot McDonald Design

Second Printing Hendrickson Publishers Edition — March 2018

Printed in the United States of America

ABOUT THE SPEAKER

Tim Pollard formerly served as Vice President of Marketing and Strategy for
Peacemaker Ministries, having come out of the corporate world as Executive Director
of a US consulting firm that specializes in the areas of strategy, marketing and
communications.

Today Tim is the founder and CEO of Oratium, a company focused on helping
for-profit companies and non-profit organizations architect deeply impactful
communications.

Tim and his wife Ruth are British by birth, but now reside in Montana where they're raising their four
kids – 2 in college and 2 in high school. He is passionate about the gospel, the church, men's ministry, and
fly-fishing.

Table of Contents

1   SESSION 1:
Facing the Flames of Conflict

7   SESSION 2:
A New Way of Thinking

11   SESSION 3:
Go to Higher Ground (Glorify God)

17   SESSION 4:
Get Real about Yourself (Get the Log out of your Eye)

23   SESSION 5:
Accepting Responsibility: Making an Effective Apology

27   SESSION 6:
Gently Engaging Others (Gently Restore)

33   SESSION 7:
Get Together on Lasting Solutions (Go and Be Reconciled)

39   SESSION 8:
Overcome Evil with Good

Because we have added valuable material to this guide to supplement the discussion and application, the actual page numbering from the original is retained so that when the speaker refers to page 12, it is in fact labeled Page 12.

Discussion questions for each Session will be labeled GROUP DISSCUSSION/1, etc; and the Bible Study section for each Session will be labeled BIBLE STUDY/1. We hope this clarifies some confusion from a previous version.

FACING

THE FLAMES

OF CONFLICT

"Healthy tensions become sinful conflicts when legitimate interests are expressed in ways that are dishonoring to God and to others."

SESSION 1
FACING THE FLAMES OF CONFLICT

▶ **PLAY VIDEO**

Why study peacemaking?

■ Conflict is all around us. It's become the "air we breathe" in our society.

■ Conflict affects our marriages, families, churches, neighborhoods and workplaces. It wears us down. It affects Christians as much as anyone else, bringing us low, damaging our relationships, and tarnishing our witness to the world.

■ But it doesn't have to be this way—there's a better way within reach of all of us. Through the good news of what Jesus did on the cross, where God reconciles a sinful people to himself, we are given both a vision and a practical way for approaching conflict differently.

■ Peacemaking brings the prospect of *hope* for broken relationships.

TWO AMAZING OBSERVATIONS

As we dig into God's Word on peacemaking, two areas of your life are going to be touched—one "past" and one "future":

1. **Past:** Many (most?) people are currently in some unreconciled relationship, and God wants to work with you in that relationship.

   Is that uncomfortable for you? For now, try to suspend your disbelief ...

2. **Future:** We lay down a new "cultural foundation" for the way we handle all the future disagreements (normal and natural) in our families, churches and workplaces.

From **selfish and destructive** to **God-glorifying and constructive**.

THE ANATOMY OF CONFLICT

"THE SPARK"

"Triggers": Where Does Conflict Come From?

- God-given *diversity* – Scripture celebrates *unity*, not *uniformity* (see 1 Cor. 12)

  ▸ Diversity leads to natural differences in preferences and priorities.

- Those inevitable *misunderstandings*

  ▸ How perfectly do we communicate?

- *Selfish attitudes* that lead to hurtful words and actions

  ▸ This comes out as anger, jealousy, gossip, etc.

  ▸ "Kids, be quiet! Can't you see I'm tired?"

These are not conflicts, but they create the opportunity for conflicts.

"THE GASOLINE"

Why Do These Differences Become Conflicts?

The problem isn't the differences, it's what we do with the differences. The root problem in conflict is the desires that battle in our hearts.

What's going on inside the *heart* *"What causes fights and quarrels among you? Don't they come from the desires that battle within you? You want something but you don't get it." James 4:1*

Definitions of an out-of-control desire (craving):

- Something you want too much (even a good thing)

- Something you will sin to obtain or sin if it's denied

- A desire that's become a demand

What kind of fires do you start when the thing you want is somehow denied?

Worldly Culture: Fuel for the Fire

- We soak in the culture of the world (a culture that is not neutral).

- What is the world's top priority? Self.

"You deserve it"   *"Because you're worth it"*

"Stick up for yourself"   *"Look out for #1"*

"Have it your way"

We are constantly bombarded by the message to care only about ourselves. ***What does the world say about selfishness? It says that it's just fine!***

What does the Bible say?

"Each of you should look not only to your own interests, but also to the interests of others." Phil. 2:4

Remember
Cravings underlie conflict.

 PAUSE FOR THOUGHT …

What are You Craving?

1. What are some of the things in your life that can become "out-of-control desires"?

2. Where have these sometimes led to conflict?

"THE FIRE"

The Destructive Effects of Conflict

- Thousands of people, including Christians, leave their jobs, neighborhoods, and friends every year due to unresolved conflict, with many people left hurting and scarred on all sides.

- Parents are estranged from children and extended family. They dread Christmas or other family gatherings because of all the unresolved conflict.

- Families are shattered and broken by divorce because of an inability or unwillingness to reconcile.

- People hate going to work and lose a huge amount of productivity because of conflict and the fear of dealing with it.

- Seemingly low-level conflict (e.g., gossip, complaining, judging, and unforgiveness) causes discouragement and drains the energy out of a workplace or family.

- People are left in despair—hurt, lonely, angry and hopeless— believing there's nowhere to turn.

Hidden on the Inside

Our Hypocrisy

When Christians fight with everyone around them, what does it say to a watching world?

Who does my boss think he is? He can't treat me like that!

After what he did, I can never forgive him!

I haven't talked to my mother in 10 years. Why am I still so angry?

I don't care what the Bible says about suing another Christian, I've got my rights!

Why did she have to leave? I told her that I'm trying to change.

IS THERE HOPE?

A Radically Different Vision for Relationships

Despite these human challenges, the Bible lays out a shockingly different vision for relationships and how we address conflict.

For our Christian relationships:

> *"By this all men will know that you are my disciples, if you love one another." John 13:35*

> *"May they be brought to complete unity **to let the world know that you sent me** and have loved them even as you have loved me." John 17:23 (emphasis added)*

> *For our relationships with the rest of the world:*

> *"Teacher, which is the greatest commandment in the Law?" Jesus replied: " 'Love the Lord your God with all your heart and with all your soul and with all your mind.' This is the first and greatest commandment. And the second is like it: '**Love your neighbor as yourself.**' " Matt. 22:36-39 (emphasis added)*

The Bible makes it abundantly clear that Jesus' desire and plan is for Christians to live in unity, loving one another *and* those around them.

But how is this possible? The answer is not, "just try hard." The power doesn't come from knowing the commands—it comes from somewhere else.

A Taste of Things to Come

> *"Be kind and compassionate to one another, forgiving each other, just as in Christ God forgave you." Eph. 4:32*

The key to extending love, mercy, and forgiveness to others is understanding the love, mercy, and forgiveness God extends to us.

Conflict as an opportunity (a good thing!)

- To look to the interests of others

- To honor one another above ourselves

- To show mercy and lay down our rights

- To reflect God's love to those around us

GROUP **DISCUSSION**

Let's talk about the two scenarios between the husband and wife in the kitchen as they discuss vacation plans …

💬 **What do you think provoked the conflict?**

💬 **Where did they go wrong?**

💬 **How did they do better in the second scenario?**

_____

_____

_____

Let's take a look at the two passages that the speaker brought up in his first message …

"Let each of you look not only to his own interests, but also to the interests of others."
(Philippians 2:4)

💬 **What is the assumption here?**

_____

_____

_____

_____

💬 **What are the two commands?**

_____

_____

_____

_____

💬 What happens when someone constantly makes his or her interests more important than the interests of others?

💬 What happens when someone constantly makes his or her interests less important than others?

💬 What may seem unnatural about putting the interests of others on the same plane of importance as our own?

Let's look at another Scripture the speaker brought up, a passage that describes how the healthy tension between legitimate interests can turn into sinful conflict.

"What causes quarrels and what causes fights among you? Is it not this, that your passions are at war within you? You desire and do not have, so you murder. You covet and cannot obtain, so you fight and quarrel. You do not have, because you do not ask." (James 4:1-2)

💬 According to this verse, why do legitimate disagreements turn into fights and quarrels?

💬 **Why do you think James uses the image of "war" to describe out-of-control desires?**

Let's talk about some real-world scenarios when we've observed simple disagreements evolve into full-blown, relationship-damaging conflicts.

However, we need to abide by this rule: The conflict you talk about cannot be with someone who is present, or someone who is not here, but we may know. It's also best not to describe an unresolved conflict with a spouse or family member (unless the story has a happy ending!).

Let's consider some questions, and you can fill in the blanks with the conflict you have in mind ...

💬 **What was the conflict about?**

_____

_____

💬 **What were the legitimate interests on both sides?**

_____

_____

💬 **How did those legitimate interests eventually become selfish desires (by one or both parties)?**

_____

_____

💬 **What emotions were expressed in the middle of the conflict by the people involved?**

_____

_____

💬 **How did the dispute end? Was there a clear winner or loser?**

_____

_____

💬 **What happened to the relationship as a result of the conflict?**

_____

_____

DAY ONE
SETTING THE STAGE

King Solomon has died, and appointed his son Rehoboam as king. Tensions are high among the tribes of Israel because Solomon had conscripted thousands of Israelites for his building projects and wore them down. The people want to know if Rehoboam is going to be like his father in this regard.

Here is the story from 1 Kings 12 …

> *Rehoboam went to Shechem, for all Israel had come to Shechem to make him king. ² And as soon as Jeroboam the son of Nebat heard of it (for he was still in Egypt, where he had fled from King Solomon), then Jeroboam returned from Egypt. ³ And they sent and called him, and Jeroboam and all the assembly of Israel came and said to Rehoboam, ⁴ "Your father made our yoke heavy. Now therefore lighten the hard service of your father and his heavy yoke on us, and we will serve you." ⁵ He said to them, "Go away for three days, then come again to me." So the people went away.*

1. What was the blossoming conflict? Who initiated the discussion?

2. Why was Rehoboam prudent not to give them an answer right away?

3. What were Rehoboam's legitimate interests?

4. What were the legitimate interests of the ten tribes of Israel?

5. What do you think Jeroboam had to gain by putting this issue on the table?

6. Why is it wise to step back and give yourself time to think when you see conflict brewing?

DAY TWO
GETTING ADVICE ...

Then King Rehoboam took counsel with the old men, who had stood before Solomon his father while he was yet alive, saying, "How do you advise me to answer this people?" ⁷ And they said to him, "If you will be a servant to this people today and serve them, and speak good words to them when you answer them, then they will be your servants forever."

⁸ But he abandoned the counsel that the old men gave him and took counsel with the young men who had grown up with him and stood before him. ⁹ And he said to them, "What do you advise that we answer this people who have said to me, 'Lighten the yoke that your father put on us'?" ¹⁰ And the young men who had grown up with him said to him, "Thus shall you speak to this people who said to you, 'Your father made our yoke heavy, but you lighten it for us,' thus shall you say to them, 'My little finger is thicker than my father's thighs. ¹¹ And now, whereas my father laid on you a heavy yoke, I will add to your yoke. My father disciplined you with whips, but I will discipline you with scorpions.'"

¹² So Jeroboam and all the people came to Rehoboam the third day, as the king said, "Come to me again the third day." ¹³ And the king answered the people harshly, and forsaking the counsel that the old men had given him, ¹⁴ he spoke to them according to the counsel of the young men, saying, "My father made your yoke heavy, but I will add to your yoke. My father disciplined you with whips, but I will discipline you with scorpions." ¹⁵ So the king did not listen to the people, for it was a turn of affairs brought about by the Lord that he might fulfill his word, which the Lord spoke by Ahijah the Shilonite to Jeroboam the son of Nebat.
(I Kings 12:6-15)

1. Why do you think Rehoboam went to two different sets of advisors?

2. What did the two views represent?

3. How did the advice of the elders address everyone's interests?

4. How did the advice of the young men only address Rehoboam's interests?

5. What was Rehoboam's final decision?

6. Where would you go for counsel when facing a conflict?

7. How do you discern between wise and foolish advice?

DAY **THREE**
THE KINGDOM DIVIDED

And when all Israel saw that the king did not listen to them, the people answered the king, "What portion do we have in David? We have no inheritance in the son of Jesse. To your tents, O Israel! Look now to your own house, David." So Israel went to their tents. ¹⁷ But Rehoboam reigned over the people of Israel who lived in the cities of Judah. ¹⁸ Then King Rehoboam sent Adoram, who was taskmaster over the forced labor, and all Israel stoned him to death with stones. And King Rehoboam hurried to mount his chariot to flee to Jerusalem. ¹⁹ So Israel has been in rebellion against the house of David to this day. ²⁰ And when all Israel heard that Jeroboam had returned, they sent and called him to the assembly and made him king over all Israel. There was none that followed the house of David but the tribe of Judah only.

²¹ When Rehoboam came to Jerusalem, he assembled all the house of Judah and the tribe of Benjamin, 180,000 chosen warriors, to fight against the house of Israel, to restore the kingdom to Rehoboam the son of Solomon. ²² But the word of God came to Shemaiah the man of God: ²³ "Say to Rehoboam the son of Solomon, king of Judah, and to all the house of Judah and Benjamin, and to the rest of the people, ²⁴ 'Thus says the Lord, You shall not go up or fight against your relatives the people of Israel. Every man return to his home, for this thing is from me.'" So they listened to the word of the Lord and went home again, according to the word of the Lord. (I Kings 12:16-24)

1. How did the ten tribes respond to their legitimate interests being ignored?

2. Did the ten tribes of Israel sin in splitting from their King, or were they just exercising a reasonable form of civil disobedience? Explain.

3. How did God demonstrate his sovereignty in the middle of this conflict?

4. What are the dangers in ignoring what is important to the person with whom you are in conflict?

DAY FOUR
WHAT HAPPENED NEXT …

Then Jeroboam built Shechem in the hill country of Ephraim and lived there. And he went out from there and built Penuel. 26 And Jeroboam said in his heart, "Now the kingdom will turn back to the house of David. 27 If this people go up to offer sacrifices in the temple of the Lord at Jerusalem, then the heart of this people will turn again to their lord, to Rehoboam king of Judah, and they will kill me and return to Rehoboam king of Judah." 28 So the king took counsel and made two calves of gold. And he said to the people, "You have gone up to Jerusalem long enough. Behold your gods, O Israel, who brought you up out of the land of Egypt." 29 And he set one in Bethel, and the other he put in Dan. 30 Then this thing became a sin, for the people went as far as Dan to be before one. 31 He also made temples on high places and appointed priests from among all the people, who were not of the Levites. 32 And Jeroboam appointed a feast on the fifteenth day of the eighth month like the feast that was in Judah, and he offered sacrifices on the altar. So he did in Bethel, sacrificing to the calves that he made. And he placed in Bethel the priests of the high places that he had made. 33 He went up to the altar that he had made in Bethel on the fifteenth day in the eighth month, in the month that he had devised from his own heart. And he instituted a feast for the people of Israel and went up to the altar to make offerings. (I Kings 12:25-33)

1. Why do people seem to drift from God when conflict is handled poorly?

2. Why is it important to make *what God wants* the top priority in conflict resolution?

3. How have you seen conflict end badly? How did it end up affecting you?

A NEW WAY OF THINKING

There are three options when it comes to conflict resolution:

1. Escape
2. Attack
3. Biblical Peacemaking

SESSION 2
A NEW WAY OF THINKING

▶ **PLAY VIDEO**

IN THE PREVIOUS SESSIONS...

- **Sparks:** Diversity, misunderstandings, selfish attitudes

- **Gasoline:** "Cravings" being challenged or denied

- **Fire:** Conflict, arguing, complaining, anger, bitterness

- **God's better way:** Love and forgive others as God loves and forgives you.

UNDERSTANDING OUR DIFFERENT RESPONSES TO CONFLICT

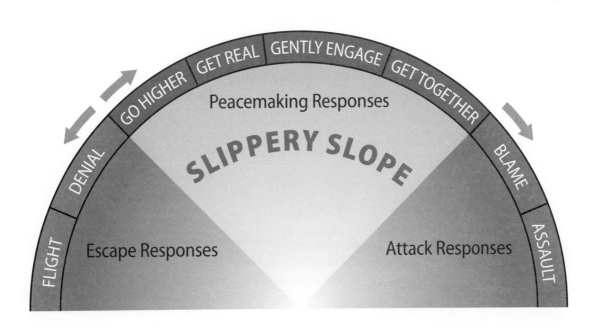

ESCAPE RESPONSES ("Running")

The responses found on the left side of the Slippery Slope are directed at getting away from the conflict rather than resolving it. These responses are:

- **Denial:** Pretend that a conflict does not exist or refuse to do what you should do to resolve it properly. This is always a wrong response to conflict.

- **Flight:** Run away from the person with whom you are having a conflict. Flight is more than escaping—it is avoiding facing a problem.

The Problem: You haven't solved anything. The issue that causes the problem comes along with you when you run away.

ATTACK RESPONSES ("Winning")

The responses found on the right side of the Slippery Slope are directed at placing as much pressure as possible on your opponent in order to win. These responses are:

- **Blame:** We attempt to shift responsibility for the conflict away from ourselves, by blaming the conflict on the other person. Blame often turns to *gossip* when we talk about others rather than speaking to them directly. Gossip seeks to win others to our side as we "try our case" in the court of public opinion by talking to lots of people.

- **Assault:** We use force or intimidation (e.g., physical, verbal, or financial) to try to make an opponent give in to our demands. We might try to force our opponents to give in to our demands by taking them to court.

> ❚❚ PAUSE FOR THOUGHT ...
> **What's Your History?**
>
> *What response to conflict did your parents typically use as you were growing up? What response do you tend to use now?*

PEACEMAKING RESPONSES

At the top of the Slope, the four principles of peacemaking focus on pursuing *reconciliation* as well as a seeking a just and mutually agreeable *resolution* to a conflict.

"The Four G's"

- **Go to Higher Ground** (*Glorify God* – 1 Cor. 10:31): This response encourages you to clarify your highest values, applying them to how you respond to conflict and treat others when experiencing conflict. For the Christian, it means asking yourself, "How can I please and honor God in this situation?"

- **Get Real About Yourself** (*Get the Log Out of Your Eye* – Matt. 7:5): This response encourages you to examine your own attitudes and actions, understanding how you have contributed to the conflict, and giving a thorough and humble confession.

- **Gently Engage Others** (*Gently Restore* – Gal. 6:1): Taking responsibility for your own contribution is followed by respectfully and graciously helping others to see how they have contributed to the conflict.

- **Get Together on Lasting Solutions** (*Go and Be Reconciled* – Matt. 5:24): Focusing on preserving and restoring the relationship through forgiveness leads you to a lasting solution that resolves both material and personal issues.

Remember
God's heart in conflict is for more than *resolution* of the issue, it's for *reconciliation* of the relationship.

A GREAT FIRST STEP: OVERLOOK IT

ASK YOURSELF, "IS THIS WORTH FIGHTING OVER?"

"A man's wisdom gives him patience; it is to his glory to overlook an offense." Proverbs 19:11

When someone has offended you, a wonderful question to ask is, "Can I overlook this?" Many conflicts can be quickly resolved if we are willing to overlook. It is an act of love to extinguish a fire before it ever starts.

Put your conflict in context. Is it a big deal in the bigger context of your life?

We are "thin-skinned" with how others treat us (i.e., we take offense easily) while we are "thick-skinned" in how we treat them (i.e., we want them to "toughen up"). A sign of maturity is to flip that around.

(*Caution:* Be sure not to fall into an "Escape" response on the Slippery Slope here. Think of overlooking as a form of **preemptive forgiveness.**)

Overlooking offenses is appropriate under three conditions.

1. The offense should not have created a wall between you and the other person or caused you to feel differently toward him or her for more than a short period of time.

2. The offense should not be causing serious harm (to God's reputation, to others, or to the offender).

3. The offense is not part of a destructive pattern.

Need for Wisdom

You don't need to overlook *all* wrongs, but ask God to help you discern and overlook *minor* wrongs.

Notes

GROUP DISCUSSION

💬 Why do some people believe if you ignore a problem long enough, it will go away? What usually happens instead?

💬 What generally happens to a problem when you run away from it? Why do the problems from which we try to escape tend to keep resurfacing?

💬 What is it about taking responsibility for a problem that can be so difficult for many people? What's at stake for them? Why does this discomfort compel some people to shift blame to others when conflict surfaces?

💬 Identify some intimidation tactics that you've either witnessed or experienced that were used to obtain unchallenged compliance.

💬 What is your conflict style? Are you more of an avoider or an attacker? Explain—give some examples, if you're willing!

The Four G's ...

G1: GO TO HIGHER GROUND

💬 **What is that God wants in regard to our relationships – not only with Him, but also with others?**

G2: GET REAL ABOUT YOURSELF

💬 **Why do you think most people have "blind spots" when it comes to their own culpability?**

G3: GENTLY ENGAGE OTHERS

💬 **What usually happens when people feel "backed into a corner" when confronted?**

G4: GET TOGETHER ON LASTING SOLUTIONS

💬 **What is the correlation between "resolution" and "relationship"? Can you have one without the other? Explain.**

(We will look at the Four G's more closely in future sessions.)

GROUP DISCUSSION

💬 **Consider the following situations in light of the three conditions listed on Video Session Page 21. Give your opinion: Overlook or Bring It Up.** Explain your responses.

Situation	Overlook	Bring it up
Neighbor blows his grass clippings onto your driveway.		
Spouse sighs audibly trying to get by you.		
Stranger leaves his grocery cart in front of your car.		
A group of teens is bullying an elementary school student.		
A passenger in your car keeps giving you driving tips.		
An extroverted co-worker talks continuously.		
A parishioner takes change from the offering plate.		

💬 **When it comes to people's idiosyncrasies, what "debts" (that they create) are you willing to simply absorb?**

_____

_____

_____

_____

💬 **When does it become unhealthy to do this?**

_____

_____

_____

_____

💬 **What is the difference between healthy "overlooking" and "peace at any price"?**

_____

_____

_____

_____

DAY ONE
THE ESCAPE RESPONSE TO CONFLICT

The "escape" response to conflict has been around for a long time – even during the infancy of the church.

Read the following account of a serious situation in the Corinthian church that the believers there were apparently avoiding.

> *For the kingdom of God does not consist in talk but in power. What do you wish? Shall I come to you with a rod, or with love in a spirit of gentleness?*
>
> *It is actually reported that there is sexual immorality among you, and of a kind that is not tolerated even among pagans, for a man has his father's wife. And you are arrogant! Ought you not rather to mourn? (1 Corinthians 4:20 – 5:2)*

1. What was the issue that the Corinthians were ignoring?

2. What possible excuses might they have been giving to just leave the situation alone?

3. Why would this situation NOT be an appropriate time to overlook an offense?

4. Why do you think the Corinthians were apparently proud of their "live and let live" attitude toward this particular man?

5. What emotional response did Paul say was appropriate to this situation?

6. What might cause you to grieve when you see obviously bad behavior that's being ignored?

DAY TWO
THE ATTACK RESPONSE TO CONFLICT

Now Abel was a keeper of sheep, and Cain a worker of the ground. ³ In the course of time Cain brought to the Lord an offering of the fruit of the ground, ⁴ and Abel also brought of the firstborn of his flock and of their fat portions. And the Lord had regard for Abel and his offering,⁵ but for Cain and his offering he had no regard. So Cain was very angry, and his face fell. ⁶ The Lord said to Cain, "Why are you angry, and why has your face fallen? ⁷ If you do well, will you not be accepted? And if you do not do well, sin is crouching at the door. Its desire is for you, but you must rule over it."

⁸ Cain spoke to Abel his brother. And when they were in the field, Cain rose up against his brother Abel and killed him. ⁹ Then the Lord said to Cain, "Where is Abel your brother?" He said, "I do not know; am I my brother's keeper?" (Genesis 4:2-9)

1. What was Cain's issue with his brother? Did Abel seem to be aware of the problem?

2. How did the Lord attempt to confront Cain's consuming desires within him?

3. What choices did Cain have in this situation? What did he end up choosing?

4. What do you think Cain and Abel talked about before Cain killed his brother?

5. How did Cain attempt to avoid accountability when he was confronted with his actions?

6. Why do some people feel tempted to resort to violence when it comes to dealing with conflict? What do they hope will happen? What usually happens instead?

DAY THREE
THE ESCAPE RESPONSE TO CONFLICT – OVERCORRECTING!

In our first study of the week, Paul was rebuking the Corinthians for turning a blind eye to open, sinful behavior among them. Now, in his second letter to them, he's telling them to hold back! Yes, they were now effectively confronting destructive behavior that they had once ignored, but now they needed to recognize that the purpose for their peacemaking had been accomplished. Once genuine repentance had been experienced, the time for reconciliation and restoration had come.

> *For I wrote to you out of much affliction and anguish of heart and with many tears, not to cause you pain but to let you know the abundant love that I have for you.*
>
> *Now if anyone has caused pain, he has caused it not to me, but in some measure—not to put it too severely—to all of you. For such a one, this punishment by the majority is enough, so you should rather turn to forgive and comfort him, or he may be overwhelmed by excessive sorrow. So I beg you to reaffirm your love for him. (2 Corinthians 2:4-8)*

1. What motivated Paul to compel the Corinthians to actively address the serious issues in their congregation instead of ignoring them?

2. What was the evidence that they had been effective in confronting this unnamed believer's destructive behaviors?

3. Why did it seem to Paul that they were taking it too far?

4. What did he want them to do instead?

5. What's the difference between authentic repentance and a half-baked apology? What will be clearly evident when genuine repentance has taken place?

6. As believers, how should we always respond to genuine repentance?

DAY FOUR
THE ESCAPE RESPONSE TO CONFLICT – AVOIDANCE!

> The Lord said [to Cain], "What have you done? The voice of your brother's blood is crying to me from the ground. [11] And now you are cursed from the ground, which has opened its mouth to receive your brother's blood from your hand. [12] When you work the ground, it shall no longer yield to you its strength. You shall be a fugitive and a wanderer on the earth." [13] Cain said to the Lord, "My punishment is greater than I can bear. [14] Behold, you have driven me today away from the ground, and from your face I shall be hidden. I shall be a fugitive and a wanderer on the earth, and whoever finds me will kill me."
> (Genesis 4:10-14)

1. Why do think Cain refused to express any remorse over murdering his brother?

2. How was the Lord going to discipline Cain for killing Abel?

3. Why is Cain overwhelmed with fear after hearing the consequences of his attack? What could he have done to address and resolve those fears?

4. Why do those who resort to violence usually find the experience hollow and dissatisfying?

5. Why do people who verbally attack those with whom they are in conflict usually find the experience empty and far less satisfying than they expected?

GO TO HIGHER GROUND (GLORIFY GOD)

God wants peaceful, flourishing relationships with His people, and between His people.

GO TO HIGHER GROUND
(GLORIFY GOD)

▶ **PLAY VIDEO**

IN THE PREVIOUS SESSIONS...

- Conflict builds up walls and tears down relationships.

- The Slippery Slope: Escape Zone, Attack Zone, and Peacemaking Zone

- The important first question: Can you overlook the offense?

INTRODUCING THE FIRST G: GO TO HIGHER GROUND (Glorify God)

"Whatever you do, do it all for the glory of God." 1 Cor. 10:31

Everyone has a set of values that they want to live by (e.g., integrity, love, respect, honesty, and truth). "Go to higher ground" simply reminds us to seek to live out those values when it really matters—like in times of conflict.

As Christians, we are called to the "high ground" of glorifying God in everything we do. But the problem we have is that we don't tend to take what we believe in church on Sundays and live it out during the rest of the week.

What Does "Glorify God" Really Mean?

- **The Corinthian context: "Have it your way."** Everyone was acting for self, and doing what was right for them. Sound familiar?

- **Paul's point: Have a "God Focus."** Ask yourself, "Where is God in this situation?" *Whatever you do*, seek to glorify God—not just on Sunday morning.

- **Practically speaking:** Obey him and imitate him by loving others showing mercy, laying down "rights," forgiving, and loving sacrificially.

The Problem of the "Horizontal Heart"

In a conflict, what is our typical focus? It's *horizontal*: we tend to look outward, not upward.

- Blame ⟷ Hurt

- What's missing from this picture? Where is God in this conflict? Remember the *vertical* dimension.

Missing Person

In most conflicts, we forget the vertical dimension:

"Where's God in this picture?"

THE "MOMENT"

We've all been there—"that moment" in a conflict—the tipping point when we can pull the pin on the grenade and make it a whole lot worse.

> "Well, maybe if you cared about being a good husband, you wouldn't leave your socks on the floor."

> "Hang on a minute! If that's your attitude, maybe you shouldn't even work here anymore."

Instead of asking "How do I win?", we can ask this question:

"What would please and honor God in this situation?"

Personal example: The Logbook

We always have a choice: run, attack, or seek to honor God. Even if you miss the first "moment," remember, *it's never too late to do the right thing.*

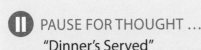

PAUSE FOR THOUGHT …
   "Dinner's Served"

Jim comes home from work. He seems sullen and distracted. Susan's had a hard day herself: she got home late from work, realized that she had forgotten to plan for dinner, and now Jim sticks his head into the kitchen wondering how much longer dinner will be.

At this pivotal moment:

A. What responses would not glorify God (and likely start a brush fire)?

B. What responses would glorify God (and be a "holy" fire extinguisher)?

Good News!
The word "gospel" literally means *good news*— the good news of all that Jesus did for us on the cross.

THE HOPE AND IMPACT OF THE GOSPEL

Definition: The gospel is the incredible news that even though we were enemies of God, alienated by our sin and deserving eternal punishment, he reached out to rescue us by sending his Son to take our punishment by dying in our place on the cross. Now through faith in Jesus, we've been reconciled to God, adopted into his family, and given a fresh start, a new life, and the supreme gift of enjoying him forever.

> *"Once you were alienated from God and were enemies in your minds because of your evil behavior. But now he has reconciled you by Christ's physical body through death to present you holy in his sight, without blemish and free from accusation." Col. 1:21-22*

> *"For God so loved the world that he gave his one and only Son, that whoever believes in him shall not perish but have eternal life." John 3:16*

Our Problem

We tend to think of the gospel only as the key to eternal life and fail to understand how completely the gospel can transform every area of our daily lives.

Throughout the New Testament, the gospel is not just the means for salvation, but it is also applied to everyday life:

> "Therefore, as God's chosen people, holy and dearly loved, clothe yourselves with compassion, kindness, humility, gentleness and patience. Bear with each other and forgive whatever grievances you may have against one another. Forgive as the Lord forgave you." Col. 3:12-13

> "[Jesus] died for all, that those who live should no longer live for themselves but for him who died for them and was raised again. Therefore, if anyone is in Christ, he is a new creation; the old has gone, the new has come!" 2 Cor. 5:15,17

THE GOSPEL CHANGES EVERYTHING!
EVERYTHING FROM FEAR TO FORGIVENESS:
The Transforming Power of the Gospel in Everyday Life

When ...	In Myself ...	But in Christ ...
I'm fearful of the future	Consumed by worry, I assume the worst and lose hope.	*Because God did not spare his son, I can trust that he walks with me and cares for me. (Rom. 8:32)*
I've fallen into sin	I cover it up, hide it, minimize it, or find someone to blame.	*Because God delights to forgive, I can freely confess my sins to him and others. (Prov. 28:13)*
Things are going well	I take pride in my achievements (and look down on lesser mortals).	*Because in Christ, all good gifts are from God, I humbly thank him and gladly share the blessing. (1 Cor. 4:7)*
Someone wrongs me	I'm bitter or angry. I fight for my rights. Estrangement. Payback.	*Because I've been forgiven, I can forgive and show mercy and compassion to others. (Eph. 4:32)*

Changed on the Inside:

It's not simply "I should." Instead, it's "I can" and eventually, "I want to."

HOW DOES THE GOSPEL AFFECT DIFFICULT RELATIONSHIPS?

Consider the story Jesus told when asked about difficult relationships:

The Unmerciful Servant: Matthew 18:21-33

Context: Peter asks Jesus, "How many times shall I forgive my brother when he sins against me?"

Scene 1: verses 24-26
- 10,000 talents owed
- Mercy asked for by servant
- Mercy granted by king

"Therefore, the kingdom of heaven is like a king who wanted to settle accounts with his servants. As he began the settlement, a man who owed him ten thousand talents was brought to him. Since he was not able to pay, the master ordered that he and his wife and his children and all that he had be sold to repay the debt. The servant fell on his knees before him. 'Be patient with me,' he begged, 'and I will pay back everything.' The servant's master took pity on him, canceled the debt and let him go.

Scene 2: verses 28-30
- 100 denarii owed
- Mercy asked for by second man
- Mercy denied by servant

"But when that servant went out, he found one of his fellow servants who owed him a hundred denarii. He grabbed him and began to choke him. 'Pay back what you owe me!' he demanded. His fellow servant fell to his knees and begged him, 'Be patient with me, and I will pay you back.' But he refused. Instead, he went off and had the man thrown into prison until he could pay the debt.

Scene 3: verses 32-33
- Jesus' conclusion
- King exercises justice on servant
- "Should you not have had mercy?"

"When the other servants saw what had happened, they were greatly distressed and went and told their master everything that had happened. Then the master called the servant in. 'You wicked servant,' he said, 'I canceled all that debt of yours because you begged me to. Shouldn't you have had mercy on your fellow servant just as I had on you?'"

Jesus' Point

The gospel—understood, appreciated and embedded—overflows all and transforms all. Because I've been forgiven, I can love and forgive.

The woman in Luke 7:39-50 was so transformed by mercy that it overflowed in her life—she couldn't contain it.

NOTE: The sum one servant owed the other servant was 100 days wages. The speaker does understate the actual value owed, not as a revision of Scripture, but as a mental comparison of the two amounts due. The difference is still quite vast whether referred to as pennies or 100 days wages when compared to the ten thousand talents owed the King, considering that 1 talent is equal to 6000 days wages.

 PAUSE FOR THOUGHT ...

"Relationships get easy in your life when the gospel gets big in your heart."

HAS THE GOSPEL CHANGED YOU IN THIS WAY?

If not, ask Jesus to dwell in you and change your mind and heart to be like his. You can't do it, but he can. God is the one who changes hearts.

> *"I will sprinkle clean water on you, and you will be clean; I will cleanse you from all your impurities and from all your idols. I will give you a new heart and put a new spirit in you; I will remove from you your heart of stone and give you a heart of flesh." Ezek. 36:25-26*

If you are struggling with conflict, remember that change doesn't come by just trying hard. It comes by asking God to let the gospel change you from the inside out.

Notes

GROUP DISCUSSION

💬 What inconsistencies did you notice in the parents' behavior when they were getting ready for church?

💬 What better example could they have set for their kids?

💬 What happens when celebrities are "glorified"? Are they "worshipped"? Put on a pedestal? Exalted as role models?

💬 Contrast this with what it means to glorify God.

💬 Describe what a "peaceful and flourishing" relationship might look like between two people.

💬 Why do you think these types of relationships are important to God? Why do you think God wants to have this type of relationship with us?

💬 How should the presence of the Holy Spirit in our hearts spill over in the ways we relate with other people?

💬 Picture yourself standing before God, where you are giving an account of a particular conflict in your life.

GROUP DISCUSSION

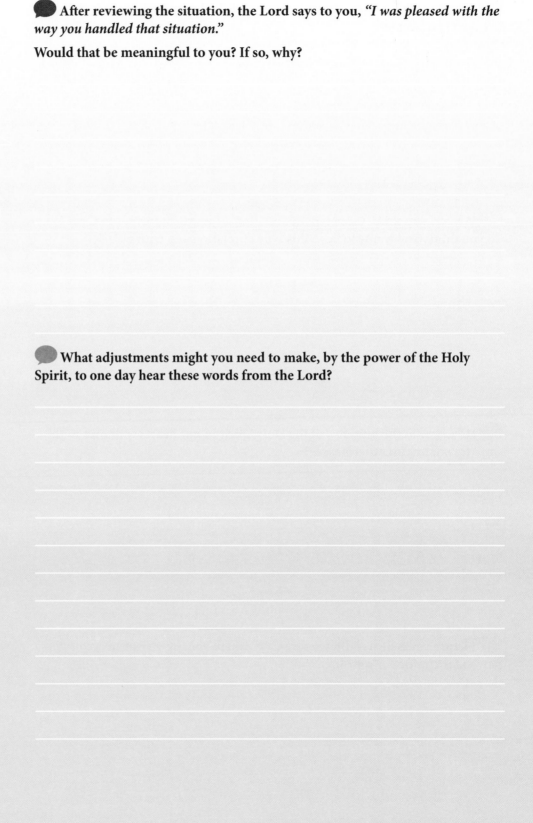

💬 After reviewing the situation, the Lord says to you, *"I was pleased with the way you handled that situation."*

Would that be meaningful to you? If so, why?

💬 **What adjustments might you need to make, by the power of the Holy Spirit, to one day hear these words from the Lord?**

DAY ONE
HOW MANY TIMES?

Then Peter came up and said to [Jesus], "Lord, how often will my brother sin against me, and I forgive him? As many as seven times?" ²² *Jesus said to him, "I do not say to you seven times, but seventy-seven times. (Matthew 18:21-22)*

1. Why do you think Peter was seeking a limit on the number of times a follower of Christ was required to forgive someone?

2. What might have been shocking to Peter about Jesus' response? Do you think Jesus literally meant more than seventy times? At what point do you think would most people lose count?

3. Why do you think Peter does not mention repentance in his question?

4. What is important about being in a state of "readiness" when it comes to facing an opportunity to forgive someone?

DAY TWO
SETTLING ACCOUNTS

"Therefore the kingdom of heaven may be compared to a king who wished to settle accounts with his servants. [24] When he began to settle, one was brought to him who owed him ten thousand talents. [25] And since he could not pay, his master ordered him to be sold, with his wife and children and all that he had, and payment to be made. [26] So the servant fell on his knees, imploring him, 'Have patience with me, and I will pay you everything.' [27] And out of pity for him, the master of that servant released him and forgave him the debt. (Matthew 18:23-27)

1. What did the servant owe the master? What were the consequences? What did the servant request of the master?

2. What does it mean to ask someone to be merciful? How is this different, if at all, from asking someone to forgive you?

3. How is God like the King in this story? Who is represented by the man who could not pay his debt?

4. What would you lose if God refused to forgive your sin?

DAY THREE
FORGETTING FORGIVENESS
....

But when that same servant went out, he found one of his fellow servants who owed him a hundred denarii, and seizing him, he began to choke him, saying, 'Pay what you owe.' [29] *So his fellow servant fell down and pleaded with him, 'Have patience with me, and I will pay you.'* [30] *He refused and went and put him in prison until he should pay the debt. (Matthew 18:28-30)*

1. How did the original servant act when he came across someone else who owed him money?

2. What exact same request did the fellow servant make of the original servant?

3. Why do you think the original servant refused to have pity on the man who owed him money?

4. What kind of debts are owed to you?

DAY FOUR ...
SHOULDN'T YOU SHOW MERCY?

When his fellow servants saw what had taken place, they were greatly distressed, and they went and reported to their master all that had taken place. ³² Then his master summoned him and said to him, 'You wicked servant! I forgave you all that debt because you pleaded with me. ³³ And should not you have had mercy on your fellow servant, as I had mercy on you?' (Matthew 18:31-33)

1. Why do you think the witnesses had such a strong emotional reaction to the servant's harsh response?

2. What was the King's reaction when he heard about the servant's heartlessness?

3. How would you contrast the seriousness of the sins against you with the sins that God has forgiven in your life? Even if that contrast is great, does that mean we are expected to dismiss the sins against us as "no big deal"? Explain your response.

4. Who serves in the role of the "witnesses" in your life? What would they report to the King about the way you respond to those who have created significant losses in your life?

GET REAL ABOUT YOURSELF

(GET THE LOG OUT OF YOUR OWN EYE)

You will gain clarity of vision when you come to terms with your contribution to the conflict – no matter how big or small it may be.

SESSION 4
GET REAL ABOUT YOURSELF
(GET THE LOG OUT OF YOUR OWN EYE)

▶ **PLAY VIDEO**

IN THE PREVIOUS SESSIONS...
The First G: Go to Higher Ground / Glorify God

- Don't leave God out of your conflicts, even when your heart wants to "go horizontal"

- "Whatever you do," seek to glorify God (especially in "the moment")

- The transforming power of the gospel

In a conflict, our hearts tend to go right to blaming the other person. Scripture teaches that we need to take a different approach.

INTRODUCING THE SECOND G:
GET REAL ABOUT YOURSELF
(Get The Log Out Of Your Eye)

"Why do you look at the speck of sawdust in your brother's eye and pay no attention to the plank in your own eye? How can you say to your brother, 'Let me take the speck out of your eye,' when all the time there is a plank in your own eye? You hypocrite, first take the plank out of your own eye, and then you will see clearly to remove the speck from your brother's eye." Matt. 7:3-5

Jesus knows we are often blind to our own faults or intentionally minimize our contribution to a conflict.

- The deadly "All I said was ..."

- Jesus doesn't forbid helping others who have a speck in their eye, but this is not where you start.

- Instead, he wants you to do something you wouldn't naturally do: ***focus <u>first</u> on your own contribution to the conflict.***

A Rule to Live By

Even if you are only responsible for 2% of a conflict, you're 100% responsible for your 2%.

The "Golden Response"

One helpful thing about "getting the log out" is that the first admission tends to trigger an admission from the other direction. *People tend to treat you the way you treat them.*

The "blame game" only escalates the situation—someone needs to break the cycle.

GETTING TO THE HEART OF CONFLICT

How do we get good at understanding our own contribution to a conflict? We must remember that ***cravings underlie conflicts.*** When we understand our hearts, we will see the cravings that are underneath conflict.

> *"What causes fights and quarrels among you? Don't they come from your desires that battle within you? You want something but don't get it. You kill and covet, but you cannot have what you want. You quarrel and fight." James 4:1-2*

It is important to get beyond the surface and get to the heart—the "why" behind the thing you did. (You may have yelled in anger, but what *caused* you to yell?) When you get down to *why* you did something, you'll see that you wanted something so much that it led to conflict.

Cravings are "idols" or "mini-gods"—things other than God that we:

- Set our hearts on (Luke 12:29)

- Let rule us (Ephesians 5:5)

- Trust, fear, or serve (Isaiah 42:17)

What Is an Idol?

An idol is:

Anything other than God that we trust to make us happy or secure.

Anger is a signal that an idol is being poked. Some common idols include: peace and quiet, obedient children, respectful co-workers, financial security, a good reputation, etc.

How Does an Idol Work?

- **Desire**: "I really would like to have a ..." (Psalm 37:4)

  All idols begin with a desire. This desire can be for anything—even something good and healthy!

- **Demand:** "I must have ..." (James 4:1)

  A desire can quickly change into a demand ("I need"). I now view the thing I want as absolutely essential.

- **Disappointment:** "You did not give me my desires ..." (Gen. 4:6-7)

  Demand leads to disappointment ("You didn't!"). Much of our disappointment in relationships is not because people have actually wronged us, but because they have failed to give us what we want.

- **Judgment:** "Because you did not give me my desires, you are ..." (Rom. 14:10)

  Frustrated at not receiving my desire, I judge, condemn, and reject those who haven't given me what I want.

- **Punishment:** "Because you didn't, I will ..." (Rom. 12:19)

  I am hurt and angry and strike back. Examples: Angry words, gossip, "giving the cold shoulder," etc.

How are you training people to give you what you want (because if they don't, you'll punish them)?

How Do I Look for Idols in My Life?

Ask "X-ray questions" to examine your heart:

■ What do you fear? What do you tend to worry about? What do you believe would bring you the greatest pain or misery?

■ What do you want? What do you believe would bring you the greatest pleasure, happiness, and delight?

■ What would you sin to obtain or sin if it's denied?

■ Have you ever "stretched" the truth in arguing for your desire (or against someone else's)?

Why is it so important to identify the idols in your life? We have the same fights over and over again because we tend to deal with our actions only at the surface level. We have to get to the root cause in order to find real change. *One thing is guaranteed: you will keep having the same conflicts if you don't uncover the idols in your heart.*

How Do I Deal with an Idol in My Heart?

The cure for an idolatrous heart is to:

■ Repent and confess the sin of idolatry and trust in God for everything you need (*Acts 3:19*).

■ Replace idol worship with worship of the true God (*Ps. 37:4*).

This is easier said than done. Our hearts are idol factories. They are always finding new things to love, have, and worship. Just trying harder isn't the answer.

"The expulsive power of a new affection ..." Thomas Chalmers

The idea here is that we drive out a "little love" with a "big love"—i.e., a growing love for God will force out the idols in our hearts. As God fills our hearts with a love for himself, we will no longer need to look to our idols for happiness or security.

CLOSING THOUGHTS

When you are addressing a conflict, always start with a "log hunt." Don't underestimate your contribution to the conflict—after all, Jesus says you've got a log (as opposed to a speck) to deal with. Honestly reflect on feedback you've received from the other person. Put yourself in their shoes. Could there be some truth to what they say?

- Read and think about God's Word related to the matter.

- Listen to the counsel of a trusted friend or pastor who will tell you the truth about yourself.

- Pray and ask God to open your eyes to any way (however seemingly small) that you may have contributed.

In a conflict, what we need is a *mirror* (to examine ourselves), but we tend to grab a *microscope* (to examine others).

GROUP DISCUSSION

💬 When something goes wrong, why do most people want to immediately assign responsibility for what happened?

Let's talk about the two workplace scenarios we watched …

💬 What were some of the "blame shifting" phrases you remember in the first scenario?

_____

_____

_____

💬 What were some of the "taking responsibility" phrases you heard in the second scenario?

_____

_____

_____

_____

💬 What's often at stake when a person considers taking responsibility for something that happened?

_____

_____

_____

_____

💬 What are some common fears associated with that decision?

_____

_____

_____

_____

💬 **Given these fears, why is it common for some people to minimize their contribution to a problem and then shift blame away from themselves?**

Despite the inner turmoil often associated with taking responsibility for our words and actions, Jesus told us that this was the first thing we must do when it comes to addressing conflict.

Let's read His teaching again …

"Why do you see the speck that is in your brother's eye, but do not notice the log that is in your own eye? Or how can you say to your brother, 'Let me take the speck out of your eye,' when there is the log in your own eye? You hypocrite, first take the log out of your own eye, and then you will see clearly to take the speck out of your brother's eye." (Matthew 7:3-5)

💬 **What does Jesus say you will be able to do if you first take responsibility for your contribution to an ongoing conflict (no matter how small)?**

This can be a hard question for some people …

Do you really want to see clearly, to understand everything that is factually true about what's behind any given conflict?
If so, then you first must look to yourself.

If not, then the core issues of any given conflict will never be resolved.

💬 **What affect will acknowledging our contribution to a problem do to the "idols" in our hearts that may be pushing us toward sinful conflict?**

GROUP DISCUSSION

💬 What kinds of desperate thoughts will these idols express in our minds in order to stay alive in our hearts?

💬 React to the following statement …
"God simply wants us to acknowledge, in our own hearts, what He can plainly see is true …"

💬 Despite the initial discomfort, why is acknowledging our contribution to a conflict such an emotionally freeing thing to do?

💬 In what ways will owning up to our words and actions free us from guilt, defensiveness, and the need to constantly justify bad decisions?

💬 Is it possible to go too far in this—to accept responsibility for issues that do not belong to you?

💬 If so, how do you know where to draw the line between responsibility that belongs to you and that which clearly belongs to someone else?

💬 When you find yourself in conflict with someone, when do you tend to get defensive?

What could this reaction be telling you?

💬 According to what we've talked about in this session, what can you do to take ownership for what truly belongs to you in any given conflict?

DAY ONE
THE PHARISEE AND THE TAX COLLECTOR

He also told this parable to some who trusted in themselves that they were righteous, and treated others with contempt: [10] *"Two men went up into the temple to pray, one a Pharisee and the other a tax collector.* [11] *The Pharisee, standing by himself, prayed thus: 'God, I thank you that I am not like other men, extortioners, unjust, adulterers, or even like this tax collector.* [12] *I fast twice a week; I give tithes of all that I get.'* [13] *But the tax collector, standing far off, would not even lift up his eyes to heaven, but beat his breast, saying, 'God, be merciful to me, a sinner!'* [14] *I tell you, this man went down to his house justified, rather than the other. For everyone who exalts himself will be humbled, but the one who humbles himself will be exalted."* (Luke 18:9-14)

1. What was the Pharisee's attitude toward the consistency of his obedience to the law? How did he contrast himself with others? How did he label those people?

2. What "label" might be applied to the Pharisee?

3. Why did you think the tax collector asked God for mercy instead of asking for forgiveness? Is there a difference? Explain.

4. For what, specifically, would you ask God for mercy?

DAY TWO
JOB'S CONFESSION

Then Job answered the Lord and said:

² "I know that you can do all things,
*   and that no purpose of yours can be thwarted.*
³ 'Who is this that hides counsel without knowledge?'
Therefore I have uttered what I did not understand,
*   things too wonderful for me, which I did not know.*
⁴ 'Hear, and I will speak;
*   I will question you, and you make it known to me.'*
⁵ I had heard of you by the hearing of the ear,
*   but now my eye sees you;*
⁶ therefore I despise myself,
*   and repent in dust and ashes."*

⁷ After the Lord had spoken these words to Job, the Lord said to Eliphaz the Temanite: "My anger burns against you and against your two friends, for you have not spoken of me what is right, as my servant Job has. ⁸ Now therefore take seven bulls and seven rams and go to my servant Job and offer up a burnt offering for yourselves. And my servant Job shall pray for you, for I will accept his prayer not to deal with you according to your folly. For you have not spoken of me what is right, as my servant Job has." ⁹ So Eliphaz the Temanite and Bildad the Shuhite and Zophar the Naamathite went and did what the Lord had told them, and the Lord accepted Job's prayer (Job 42:1-9)

1. How did Job express his repentance to God? What seemed to be Job's underlying problem that had now been fully acknowledged by his confession?

2. What do you think is the significance of dust and ashes as a symbol of genuine repentance? What could those symbols represent?

3. In what ways did the Lord vindicate Job after the suffering man's confession?

4. How does suffering, or difficult circumstances, tend to "squeeze" things to the surface so that you can deal with them?

DAY THREE
PAUL'S CONFESSION

For I do not understand my own actions. For I do not do what I want, but I do the very thing I hate. [16] Now if I do what I do not want, I agree with the law, that it is good. [17] So now it is no longer I who do it, but sin that dwells within me. [18] For I know that nothing good dwells in me, that is, in my flesh. For I have the desire to do what is right, but not the ability to carry it out. [19] For I do not do the good I want, but the evil I do not want is what I keep on doing. [20] Now if I do what I do not want, it is no longer I who do it, but sin that dwells within me.

[21] So I find it to be a law that when I want to do right, evil lies close at hand. [22] For I delight in the law of God, in my inner being, [23] but I see in my members another law waging war against the law of my mind and making me captive to the law of sin that dwells in my members. [24] Wretched man that I am! Who will deliver me from this body of death? [25] Thanks be to God through Jesus Christ our Lord! So then, I myself serve the law of God with my mind, but with my flesh I serve the law of sin. (Romans 7:15-25)

1. What seemed to be a constant tension in Paul's heart?

2. In what sense does Paul acknowledge his inability to deal with this tension, at least under his own power?

3. What role does the Holy Spirit play when it comes to genuine repentance?

4. What are some of the consistent tensions with which you struggle? How might you be able to overcome those challenges by the power of the Holy Spirit?

DAY FOUR
DAVID'S CONFESSION

Have mercy on me, O God,
*   according to your steadfast love;*
according to your abundant mercy
*   blot out my transgressions.*
² Wash me thoroughly from my iniquity,
*   and cleanse me from my sin!*

³ For I know my transgressions,
*   and my sin is ever before me.*
⁴ Against you, you only, have I sinned
*   and done what is evil in your sight,*
so that you may be justified in your words
*   and blameless in your judgment.*
⁵ Behold, I was brought forth in iniquity,
*   and in sin did my mother conceive me.*
⁶ Behold, you delight in truth in the inward being,
*   and you teach me wisdom in the secret heart.*

⁷ Purge me with hyssop, and I shall be clean;
*   wash me, and I shall be whiter than snow.*
⁸ Let me hear joy and gladness;
*   let the bones that you have broken rejoice.*
⁹ Hide your face from my sins,
*   and blot out all my iniquities.*
¹⁰ Create in me a clean heart, O God,
*   and renew a right spirit within me.*
¹¹ Cast me not away from your presence,
*   and take not your Holy Spirit from me.*
¹² Restore to me the joy of your salvation,
*   and uphold me with a willing spirit.*

¹³ Then I will teach transgressors your ways,
*   and sinners will return to you.*
¹⁴ Deliver me from bloodguiltiness, O God,
*   O God of my salvation,*
*   and my tongue will sing aloud of your righteousness.*
¹⁵ O Lord, open my lips,
*   and my mouth will declare your praise.*
¹⁶ For you will not delight in sacrifice, or I would give it;
*   you will not be pleased with a burnt offering.*
¹⁷ The sacrifices of God are a broken spirit;
*   a broken and contrite heart, O God, you will not despise.*

¹⁸ Do good to Zion in your good pleasure;
*   build up the walls of Jerusalem;*
¹⁹ then will you delight in right sacrifices,
*   in burnt offerings and whole burnt offerings;*
*   then bulls will be offered on your altar.*
*   (Psalm 51)*

1. What are all the requests that David makes of God in this psalm?

2. What is David willing to acknowledge?

3. In what sense is sinning against others really sinning against God?

4. Rewrite this psalm with your own transgressions in mind.

Session 5

ACCEPTING RESPONSIBILITY

MAKING AN EFFECTIVE APOLOGY

Clearly acknowledging and owning up to your contribution to the conflict (no matter how big or small) models the response you'd like to see from the other person.

SESSION 5
ACCEPTING RESPONSIBILITY
MAKING AN EFFECTIVE APOLOGY

▶ **PLAY VIDEO**

IN THE PREVIOUS SESSIONS…

- The power of the gospel: What Jesus did changes everything.

- The First G: Go to Higher Ground / Glorify God

- The Second G: Get Real About Yourself / Get the Log Out of Your Eye

  ▸ Don't focus on the other person—start with what you did.

  ▸ Look for your idols and remove with "the expulsive power of a new affection."

So you realize you need to apologize in obedience to Jesus' command in Matthew 7:5. But what does that look like?

It's amazing how hard it is to make a good apology. Bad apologies are what naturally come out of our mouths.

"Look, I'm sorry, OK?"

"I'm sorry, I didn't realize you were so sensitive."

Instead of helping, a bad apology will make the conflict worse.

An apology or confession is *not* about escaping the consequences or "moving on." Instead, it's about healing a hurt or restoring the wounded.

MAKING A GOOD CONFESSION: THE "7 A'S"

"He who conceals his sins does not prosper; but whoever confesses and renounces them finds mercy." Prov. 28:13

ADDRESS everyone involved (Ps. 41:4; Luke 19:8). The confession should go as far as the offense.

AVOID ifs and buts (Ps. 51). These words ruin your confession. "If" means "I really don't think I did anything wrong." "But" blames it on someone else and cancels out everything you just confessed!

ADMIT specifically. We love to be vague about ourselves (but amazingly specific about others)! Confess both your specific actions and underlying attitude.

ACKNOWLEDGE the hurt. Express understanding and genuine sorrow for the way you affected that person. (Do not assume you understand the pain—always check.)

ACCEPT the consequences (Luke 19:8). A willingness to accept the consequences is often the mark of a genuine confession.

ALTER (change) your behavior (Eph. 4:22-32). Explain how, with God's help, you plan to change.

- An apology is like a promise—words are tied to future actions.
- This helps you go beyond, "I'm sorry I got caught."

ASK for forgiveness (Gen. 50:17). This gives the offended person the opportunity to respond and express forgiveness.

Caution!
Don't turn the "7 A's" into a check list.

THREE FINAL REFLECTIONS

Remember to allow time. When we confess, the other person may sometimes forgive us immediately. But other times, they may not be ready to grant forgiveness on the spot. You may need to allow additional time for someone to process your confession. (And if you are the offended one, don't withhold forgiveness as a form of punishment.)

Don't use your confession to point out sin in others. Even if the other person has a contribution, this is not the time to deal with it. Stay focused on yourself and your own contribution.

Are you really sorry? *It's quite possible to do the 7A's and not be sorry at all.* The 7A's are not sorrow themselves, but are merely an expression of sorrow. Ask God to change your heart to be genuinely sorrowful for the hurt you've caused others and for your offense against God.

Let's review some of the expressions of regret from the "Bad Apology Hall of Fame."

THE APOLOGY	*"The comment was not meant to be a regional slur. To the extent that it was misinterpreted to be one, I apologize."*
THE OFFENSE	An attorney, apologizing for referring to potential jurors as "illiterate cave dwellers."
THE APOLOGY	*"I did not pay enough attention to detail or to the way some of my actions could have been perceived and my personal style could have been perceived by certain people."*
THE OFFENSE	A nonprofit executive, apologizing for the outrageously lavish "perks" he received.
THE APOLOGY	*"If anything I have said has hurt Billy or his family, I apologize. But I don't apologize for my opinion."*
THE OFFENSE	A country music singer, after he criticized another singer's popular song.
THE APOLOGY	*"It was an unfortunate remark that once it's in print it looks a lot worse than it actually is."*
THE OFFENSE	A politician, apologizing for calling his rival "an unusually good liar."
THE APOLOGY	*"I want everyone to know how sorry I am for what happened. I'm not as bad as everyone has made me out to be. Yes, I was wrong, but I didn't kill anybody."*
THE OFFENSE	A professional athlete, apologizing after attacking his coach during a team practice.

💬 What struck you about Marion Jones's confession in the video? What may have convinced you that it was genuine?

💬 If someone caused a significant loss in your life, felt deeply remorseful, and wanted to be reconciled with you, what would have to happen for you to fully trust that person again?

💬 What makes an apology "less than believable" to you? How do you usually feel after receiving one these—followed by a request for blanket forgiveness?

💬 Do you trust some people more than you do others? If so, on what basis do you decide this?

💬 Why does making a specific, effective apology increase your trustworthiness?

One of the purposes of making an effective apology is to model how you would like the other person to respond in regard to his or her contribution to the conflict.

💬 **Address Everyone Involved:** Why do you think it's important to address the concerns of everyone who may have been impacted by your words and actions? What are some common reasons to avoid doing this?

💬 **Avoid "ifs" and "buts":** Why does qualifying or blame-shifting always discredit the apologies in which they are wrapped?

💬 **Admit Specifically:** Why do blanket apologies seem to water down an offender's admission? What can people avoid (or deny later) by not being specific? Why do you think it is important to clearly identify what was actually said or done when it comes to confession?

💬 **Acknowledge the Hurt:** What tends to happen to a person's level of defensiveness when he or she hears an acknowledgment of the losses that person has suffered caused by the conflict?

GROUP DISCUSSION

💬 **Accept the Consequences:** Why does restitution, even when it's just symbolic, have a such a powerful effect on someone who's been hurt?

💬 **Alter (Change) Your Behavior:** Why is reconciliation dependent upon a high confidence that the conflict-provoking behaviors are not going to be repeated?

💬 **Ask for Forgiveness:** Why do all the previous steps "set the stage" for reconciliation?

💬 Is there someone with whom you can go through these steps this week? If so, call that person and set up a time to meet.

On Your Own

Here are four days of Bible studies that you can do on your own that will take you a little deeper into the nature of conflict …these reflect different degrees of deflecting responsibility instead of apologizing for what happened.

DAY ONE
ADAM AND EVE

And they heard the sound of the Lord God walking in the garden in the cool of the day, and the man and his wife hid themselves from the presence of the Lord God among the trees of the garden. ⁹ But the Lord God called to the man and said to him, "Where are you?"¹⁰ And he said, "I heard the sound of you in the garden, and I was afraid, because I was naked, and I hid myself." ¹¹ He said, "Who told you that you were naked? Have you eaten of the tree of which I commanded you not to eat?" ¹² The man said, "The woman whom you gave to be with me, she gave me fruit of the tree, and I ate." ¹³ Then the Lord God said to the woman, "What is this that you have done?" The woman said, "The serpent deceived me, and I ate." (Genesis 3:8-13)

1. Why do you think Adam and Eve tried to hide from God after they sinned? Why did that prove to be futile?

2. Whom did Adam blame for his sin? How did he even try to put some of that responsibility on to God? Why does that never work?

3. Whom did Eve try to blame for her sin? Even though she was tempted and deceived by an outside evil influence, was she still morally responsible for acting on that temptation? Explain.

4. In what ways have you tried to hide from God after you've sinned? How has that proven to be futile?

DAY TWO
AM I MY BROTHER'S KEEPER?

In the course of time Cain brought to the Lord an offering of the fruit of the ground, ⁴ and Abel also brought of the firstborn of his flock and of their fat portions. And the Lord had regard for Abel and his offering,⁵ but for Cain and his offering he had no regard. So Cain was very angry, and his face fell. ⁶ The Lord said to Cain, "Why are you angry, and why has your face fallen? ⁷ If you do well, will you not be accepted? And if you do not do well, sin is crouching at the door. Its desire is for you, but you must rule over it."

⁸ Cain spoke to Abel his brother. And when they were in the field, Cain rose up against his brother Abel and killed him. ⁹ Then the Lord said to Cain, "Where is Abel your brother?" He said, "I do not know; am I my brother's keeper?" ¹⁰ And the Lord said, "What have you done? The voice of your brother's blood is crying to me from the ground. (Genesis 4:3-10)

1. How did God try to warn Cain about the power of sin lurking at the door of his heart?

2. How do we know that Cain had ignored God's warning? What might have been different if Cain had taken God seriously?

3. How did Cain try to deflect attention away from his responsibility for murdering his brother? What evidence did God present to refute Cain's claims?

4. What evidence might God present in response to our attempts to deflect responsibility for our damaging words and actions? What's a better response instead?

DAY THREE
THE RICH MAN AND LAZARUS

"There was a rich man who was clothed in purple and fine linen and who feasted sumptuously every day.[20] And at his gate was laid a poor man named Lazarus, covered with sores, [21] who desired to be fed with what fell from the rich man's table. Moreover, even the dogs came and licked his sores. [22] The poor man died and was carried by the angels to Abraham's side. The rich man also died and was buried, [23] and in Hades, being in torment, he lifted up his eyes and saw Abraham far off and Lazarus at his side. [24] And he called out, 'Father Abraham, have mercy on me, and send Lazarus to dip the end of his finger in water and cool my tongue, for I am in anguish in this flame.' [25] But Abraham said, 'Child, remember that you in your lifetime received your good things, and Lazarus in like manner bad things; but now he is comforted here, and you are in anguish. [26] And besides all this, between us and you a great chasm has been fixed, in order that those who would pass from here to you may not be able, and none may cross from there to us.' [27] And he said, 'Then I beg you, father, to send him to my father's house— [28] for I have five brothers—so that he may warn them, lest they also come into this place of torment.' [29] But Abraham said, 'They have Moses and the Prophets; let them hear them.' [30] And he said, 'No, father Abraham, but if someone goes to them from the dead, they will repent.' [31] He said to him, 'If they do not hear Moses and the Prophets, neither will they be convinced if someone should rise from the dead.'" (Luke 16:19-31)

1. What was the rich man's sin?

2. Why do you think the rich man never addressed Lazarus, but only Abraham? In what sense was the rich man still treating Lazarus as if the former beggar was "below" him?

3. What is striking about the rich man's complete lack of remorse, even in his state of torment?

4. Is it possible that there dwells within you certain insensitivities to which you are unaware? Who could you ask to help you root these out?

DAY FOUR
DIOTREOPHES VS. DEMETRIUS

I have written something to the church, but Diotrephes, who likes to put himself first, does not acknowledge our authority. [10] So if I come, I will bring up what he is doing, talking wicked nonsense against us. And not content with that, he refuses to welcome the brothers, and also stops those who want to and puts them out of the church.

[11] Beloved, do not imitate evil but imitate good. Whoever does good is from God; whoever does evil has not seen God. [12] Demetrius has received a good testimony from everyone, and from the truth itself. We also add our testimony, and you know that our testimony is true. (3 John 1:9-12)

1. What was Diotrephes' motive behind refusing to acknowledge the authority of the apostles?

2. How did his defiance manifest itself in his actions?

3. What is the contrast between Diotrephes and Demetrius?

4. In what ways are you like Diotrephes? Demetrius? Explain.

GENTLY ENGAGE OTHERS

(GENTLY RESTORE)

Clearly communicating how another person's words and actions have impacted you sets the stage for deeper levels of reconciliation.

SESSION 6
GENTLY ENGAGE OTHERS
(GENTLY RESTORE)

▶ **PLAY VIDEO**

IN THE PREVIOUS SESSIONS...

- The gospel changes everything. It gives us the *power* and *motivation* to be different.

- The First G: Go to Higher Ground / Glorify God

- Don't forget God when you are in a conflict. Ask yourself, "What would please and honor God in this situation?"

- The Second G: Get Real About Yourself / Get the Log Out of Your Eye

  ▸ Start with yourself and your own contribution (idols)

  ▸ The heart of a great confession (7 A's)

INTRODUCING THE THIRD G: GENTLY ENGAGE OTHERS
(Gently Restore)

"Brothers, if someone is caught in a sin, you who are spiritual should restore him gently." Gal. 6:1

Many times, you don't get here—remember that when you take responsibility for your contribution, the other person often will, too (the "Golden Response").

As Christians, we are sometimes also called to help others see their contribution to a conflict. But the way we do that is critical.

The Big Misunderstanding

Even though the world's best known Bible verse is "Judge not lest you be judged," we are not prohibited from pointing out hurtful actions or attitudes in others. Instead, we *must* go to the other person gently in order to restore their relationship with God and with the people they've hurt; the purpose is *redemptive*.

A different perspective:

> *"Nothing is so cruel as the tenderness that consigns another to his sin. Nothing can be more compassionate than the severe rebuke that calls a brother back from the path of sin."*
>
> Dietrich Bonhoeffer, *Life Together*

Reminder
Before you go to someone else, remember that overlooking the offense is still an option (see pages 9-10).

Correcting others is an act of *love*—pulling someone away from the cliff—but it must be done in the right way.

The Third G is NOT:	The Third G IS:
■ Just confronting someone (if you want to confront someone, it might be a bad idea)	■ Going with a heart of love for the other person
■ Going in a spirit of anger or vengeance ("don't correct sin in sin")	■ Going with the goal of a restored relationship between the two of you
■ Going to "ding" them in a self-righteous spirit	■ Going to lead them away from the cliff edge of sin
	■ Going gently

The governing dynamic is love. A rule of thumb should be to go in love or don't go at all.

Remember the Golden Rule: Treat others the way you would like to be treated yourself (see Luke 6:31).

How do I go?

In Matthew 18, Jesus gives us practical steps to follow to gently restore a brother or sister.

Important Rule:

Keep it as private as possible as long as possible.

STEP ONE: GO TALK TO THEM

Go when there's a problem … and go in private.

> *"If your brother sins against you, go and show him his fault, just between the two of you. If he listens to you, you have won your brother over." Matt. 18:15*

Things to remember as you go:

- Sooner or later you need to talk face-to-face. Use phone calls, letters, and (especially!) e-mails sparingly.

- Be quick to listen. Draw the other person out. Remember, you do not know their heart. You may see *"what"* but you don't see *"why."* Ask more questions (and make fewer statements).

- Bring hope through the gospel. Don't just leave someone feeling condemned; show them the *hope* we all have in the gospel to receive forgiveness and to change.

STEP TWO: GET HELP

> *"But if he will not listen, take one or two others along, so that every matter may be established by the testimony of two or three witnesses." Matt. 18:16*

If you are having trouble resolving the conflict just between the two of you, Jesus says it is appropriate to involve others so that they can help you both. It's not to gang up on the other person, though.

(Obviously it's best if both of you agree to ask someone else to help you, but if necessary, you may need to take the initiative to involve others in the process.)

The Benefits of Getting Help with Your Conflict

- In an emotional situation, having an outsider present helps everyone to be more loving and careful in their communication.

- While the third party is not there to "judge" who is right or wrong, they can ask questions and actually help you both to understand facts and feelings better.

- They may apply *gentle* pressure to help someone caught in sin move to repentance (again, with the purpose being restoration).

- A godly person can help open your eyes to what God's Word says about your conflict.

Don't Forget Your Church!

When you are looking for help, one of the first places you should look is in your church. It's easy to feel alone when you are in a serious conflict, but that's the time when a wise and godly church leader can step in and offer help. It may be tough to get past your pride, but make the effort to reach out for help from your church (particularly if you are struggling in your marriage, but even for conflicts at work).

Many churches have developed "peacemaking teams" that are specifically created to help when their members are struggling with all types of conflict. For information on these teams and how to get one started in your church, please visit **www.peacemaker.net/teams**.

HAVING THAT DIFFICULT CONVERSATION

Two settings for using this tool:

1. When you are going to point out a sin in others (or other hard conversations)

2. When resolving the *material issue* in a conflict (e.g., where to go on vacation, how much money is owed, or who gets Grandma's piano)

The "PAUSE Principle" is a great tool to use to help us have God-glorifying conversations in both situations.

The PAUSE Principle
Gently engaging to deal with the material issue

> *"Do nothing out of selfish ambition or vain conceit, but in humility consider others better than yourselves. Each of you should look not only to your own interests, but also to the interests of others." Phil. 2:3-4*

PREPARE. (See Prov. 14:8) Think ahead about this conversation and what you can do in advance to make it go well.

- Pray

- Seek godly counsel

- Study Scripture

- Develop options, plan an alternative

- Plan your remarks

- Anticipate reactions

AFFIRM **relationships.** Every conflict involves both **people** and a **problem.** Focusing on the problem and not the people makes things worse. So make sure that the other person knows that you value the relationship.

UNDERSTAND interests. Take time to understand what the other person really wants and cares about. (See Phil. 2:1-4)

- **Interest**: What really motivates people and gives rise to their position. An *interest* may be a concern, desire, need, limitation, or something a person values or fears. It's the underlying thing they are trying to accomplish.

SEARCH for creative solutions. Don't get stuck on only two choices. (See Prov. 14:8)

EVALUATE options objectively and reasonably. Include a specific step in the process that checks how the solution is working. (See Dan. 1:11-16)

Notes

GROUP DISCUSSION

💬 What did you think of the "Sin Police"?

💬 Have you ever been a victim, or an "officer," of the Sin Police? Explain.

💬 To the best of your understanding, explain the importance of modeling acknowledgement and genuine repentance before asking someone else to do that.

💬 What should you do if the "golden response" doesn't happen, and the person to whom you've confessed doesn't reciprocate?

💬 What might cause a person to become defensive when you broach the subject of personal responsibility?

💬 What kinds of things can you say or do to help the person you are confronting not feel like he or she is being backed into a corner?

💬 What are some unhealthy motives for wanting to confront someone—or get someone to acknowledge his or her contribution to a conflict?

💬 What's the only God-honoring motive for taking the step of loving confrontation?

💬 Do you believe that you can accurately judge a person's motives? Explain.

💬 Why are "guessed motives" often easily denied by the person to whom those intentions are attributed?

GROUP DISCUSSION

💬 Why is it better to focus on what someone actually said or did, and how those words and actions impacted you, than to try to attribute motives to their actions?

💬 Why is it important to communicate the priority of the relationship over the resolution of the issue?

💬 Why do the intense emotions that often energize conflict diminish significantly when you first ask the other person to describe his or her perception of what's going on?

💬 Why does involving mature believers in a conflict at the right time often help to move everyone involved toward resolution? What characteristics should these peacemakers have?

💬 Describe how each step of the PAUSE Principle might be applied to a conflict you currently find yourself in.

DAY ONE
REUBEN AND GAD

Now the people of Reuben and the people of Gad had a very great number of livestock. And they saw the land of Jazer and the land of Gilead, and behold, the place was a place for livestock. ² So the people of Gad and the people of Reuben came and said to Moses and to Eleazar the priest and to the chiefs of the congregation,³ "Ataroth, Dibon, Jazer, Nimrah, Heshbon, Elealeh, Sebam, Nebo, and Beon, ⁴ the land that the Lord struck down before the congregation of Israel, is a land for livestock, and your servants have livestock." ⁵ And they said, "If we have found favor in your sight, let this land be given to your servants for a possession. Do not take us across the Jordan." (Numbers 32:1-5)

1. What did the tribes of Reuben and Gad want from Moses?

2. What were the reasons they gave?

3. Did they have legitimate interests in making this request? Explain.

4. How did they make their request in a way that demonstrated honor and respect for those who could grant their petition?

DAY TWO
MOSES RESPONDS

But Moses said to the people of Gad and to the people of Reuben, "Shall your brothers go to the war while you sit here? [7] *Why will you discourage the heart of the people of Israel from going over into the land that the Lord has given them?* [8] *Your fathers did this, when I sent them from Kadesh-barnea to see the land.* [9] *For when they went up to the Valley of Eshcol and saw the land, they discouraged the heart of the people of Israel from going into the land that the Lord had given them.* [10] *And the Lord's anger was kindled on that day, and he swore, saying,* [11] *'Surely none of the men who came up out of Egypt, from twenty years old and upward, shall see the land that I swore to give to Abraham, to Isaac, and to Jacob, because they have not wholly followed me,* [12] *none except Caleb the son of Jephunneh the Kenizzite and Joshua the son of Nun, for they have wholly followed the Lord.'* [13] *And the Lord's anger was kindled against Israel, and he made them wander in the wilderness forty years, until all the generation that had done evil in the sight of the Lord was gone.* [14] *And behold, you have risen in your fathers' place, a brood of sinful men, to increase still more the fierce anger of the Lord against Israel!* [15] *For if you turn away from following him, he will again abandon them in the wilderness, and you will destroy all this people." (Numbers 32:6-15)*

1. What objections did Moses voice?

2. What historical precedents did Moses raise?

3. What parallels did Moses draw between those who rebelled against God in the wilderness with the tribes of Reuben and Gad?

4. What was not so "gentle" about Moses' response? Why do you think his response was so impassioned?

DAY THREE
THE EXPLANATION

Then they came near to him and said, "We will build sheepfolds here for our livestock, and cities for our little ones, ¹⁷ but we will take up arms, ready to go before the people of Israel, until we have brought them to their place. And our little ones shall live in the fortified cities because of the inhabitants of the land. ¹⁸ We will not return to our homes until each of the people of Israel has gained his inheritance. ¹⁹ For we will not inherit with them on the other side of the Jordan and beyond, because our inheritance has come to us on this side of the Jordan to the east." ²⁰ So Moses said to them, "If you will do this, if you will take up arms to go before the Lord for the war, ²¹ and every armed man of you will pass over the Jordan before the Lord, until he has driven out his enemies from before him ²² and the land is subdued before the Lord; then after that you shall return and be free of obligation to the Lord and to Israel, and this land shall be your possession before the Lord. ²³ But if you will not do so, behold, you have sinned against the Lord, and be sure your sin will find you out. ²⁴ Build cities for your little ones and folds for your sheep, and do what you have promised." ²⁵ And the people of Gad and the people of Reuben said to Moses, "Your servants will do as my lord commands. ²⁶ Our little ones, our wives, our livestock, and all our cattle shall remain there in the cities of Gilead, ²⁷ but your servants will pass over, every man who is armed for war, before the Lord to battle, as my lord orders." (Numbers 32:16-27)

1. What was the misunderstanding in regard to the intentions of Reuben and Gad?

2. What could the two tribes have made a bit clearer in the beginning?

3. How did Moses respond to their clarification?

4. Why is it important to ask clarifying questions before you jump to conclusions?

DAY FOUR
THE SOLUTION

[28] So Moses gave command concerning them to Eleazar the priest and to Joshua the son of Nun and to the heads of the fathers' houses of the tribes of the people of Israel. [29] And Moses said to them, "If the people of Gad and the people of Reuben, every man who is armed to battle before the Lord, will pass with you over the Jordan and the land shall be subdued before you, then you shall give them the land of Gilead for a possession. [30] However, if they will not pass over with you armed, they shall have possessions among you in the land of Canaan." [31] And the people of Gad and the people of Reuben answered, "What the Lord has said to your servants, we will do. [32] We will pass over armed before the Lord into the land of Canaan, and the possession of our inheritance shall remain with us beyond the Jordan."
(Numbers 32:28-32)

1. What conditions did Moses place on the two tribes in granting their request?

2. What would the consequences be if they failed to uphold their end of the agreement?

3. How did the final solution turn out to be mutually beneficial to both sides of the conflict?

4. Why do you think it's important for the resolution of any conflict to clearly address what's important to everyone involved?

GET TOGETHER

ON LASTING

SOLUTIONS

(GO AND BE RECONCILED)

When the relationship is given top billing, mutually beneficial solutions to issues are often easier to find.

SESSION 7
GET TOGETHER ON LASTING SOLUTIONS
(GO AND BE RECONCILED)

▶ **PLAY VIDEO**

IN THE PREVIOUS SESSIONS...

■ The First G: Go to Higher Ground / Glorify God

■ The Second G: Get Real About Yourself / Get the Log Out of Your Eye

■ The Third G: Gently Engage Others / Gently Restore

  ▸ Go talk to them (in private); Get help

  ▸ The PAUSE Principle (having those difficult conversations)

INTRODUCING THE FOURTH G:
GET TOGETHER ON LASTING SOLUTIONS
(Go and Be Reconciled)

It is important to remember that a lasting solution will always be a combination of the *resolution of the issue* and the *reconciliation of the relationship*. If you only resolve the issue, the solution will never last.

The only hope for ongoing peace after a conflict is to seek a *reconciled relationship*, which comes through the incredible act of forgiveness.

THE TRICKY TOPIC OF FORGIVENESS

"Therefore, if you are offering your gift at the altar and there remember that your brother has something against you, leave your gift there in front of the altar. First go and be reconciled to your brother then come and offer your gift." Matt. 5:23-24

- "Being reconciled" is the giving and receiving of true heart forgiveness.

- It should be the hallmark of the Christian. Why? Because we are the most *forgiven* people in the world, we can and should be the most *forgiving*.

- However, forgiveness is hard. Many people, including Christians, still struggle with bitterness and unforgiveness.

- Forgiveness raises some interesting (and complicated) questions like, "What does 'I forgive you' really mean?" or "Do I forgive someone who has not repented?" or "What about the consequences?"

UNPACKING FORGIVENESS

What forgiveness is not:

Forgiveness is neither a feeling, nor forgetting, nor is it excusing.

What forgiveness is:

Forgiveness is a <u>decision</u> modeled after God's forgiveness of us—a decision not to hold an offense against the offender.

"Be kind and compassionate to one another, forgiving each other, just as in Christ God forgave you." Eph. 4:32

Remember This

Forgiveness isn't a matter of whether we forget, but of how we remember.

FORGIVENESS DEFINED: A TWO-STAGE PROCESS

How does it work?

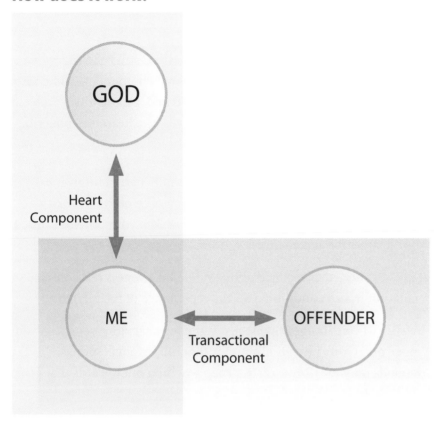

The Heart Component of Forgiveness

The heart component is the releasing of the offense to God. It is between you and God, and it is not conditional on the repentance of the other person. It is a "disposition." This component is wonderfully expressed in the following quote:

> "When we strive against all thoughts of revenge; when we will not do our enemies mischief, but wish well to them, grieve at their calamities, pray for them, seek reconciliation with them, and show ourselves ready on all occasions to relieve them. This is gospel forgiving."
>
> *Thomas Watson*

This heart component will help to protect you from developing a root of bitterness that can poison your heart. It's a readiness to extend forgiveness and enjoy reconciliation when the other person is ready to repent.

Reminder
Unforgiveness is the poison **we** drink hoping **someone else** will die.

The Transactional Component of Forgiveness

Granting forgiveness to the offender is conditional on the repentance of the offender. When the other person confesses, you can extend forgiveness, releasing them from the offense and enjoying a fully restored relationship.

But what if the offender is not repentant? Do you still need to forgive them? That's where these heart and transactional components come into play: regardless whether the offender has repented, we can always release the offense and maintain a readiness to forgive—the heart component.

Is Heart Forgiveness Real?

Yes! Heart forgiveness is real forgiveness. It is not "partial forgiveness," or "forgiveness lite." It is complete for you. As you've obeyed Christ's command to "forgive from the heart" (Matt. 18:35), your burden is lifted and your disposition has changed.

What is not complete is reconciliation. While forgiveness rests on you, reconciliation is also conditional on the repentance of the offender.

But beware of one danger: Don't just settle for heart forgiveness so you can "move on." God's heart is always for that full reconciliation, so "as far as it depends on you" (Rom. 12:18), keep reaching out towards that goal.

WHAT DOES "I FORGIVE YOU" REALLY MEAN?

Forgiveness is Four Promises:

With God's help:

- "I promise I will not dwell on this incident." (H)

- "I promise I will not bring up this incident and use it against you." (T)

- "I promise I will not talk to others about this incident." (T)

- "I promise I will not allow this incident to stand between us or hinder our personal relationship." (T)

Note
The Heart (H) and Transactional (T) components of forgiveness are also connected to the Four Promises.

WHAT ABOUT THE CONSEQUENCES?

True heart forgiveness does not necessarily release us from the worldly consequences of our sin.

If someone has wronged you, it takes wisdom to determine whether or not to enforce a set of consequences:

- Sometimes it is best to show mercy

- Sometimes it is best to allow a person to experience consequences that will teach a needed lesson

It all depends on what will most effectively serve the other person and glorify God.

Examples:

- A man confesses to embezzling from a neighborhood organization

- A teen breaks a household rule for use of the cell phone

Can they be forgiven? Yes. Are there still consequences? Yes.

Remember, the essence of the fourth promise is that you should never let the consequence be *relational*.

RECONCILIATION TAKES WORK

Is Forgiveness Hard?

- Yes. In forgiving, we lay down our rights to justice, to money, or to something else valuable. Forgiveness costs us something. The debt is real. In this sense, forgiveness is suffering in a real way. However, ask this: "Where has the punishment already been paid?" **On the cross of Christ**.

- Reflect again on how much you have been forgiven (remember the parable of the unmerciful servant in Matt. 18).

- Realize that you can't ultimately forgive in your own strength. Only God can give us the desire and ability to truly forgive others' sins (see Phil. 2:13).

Consider the following testimony from Corrie Ten Boom:

 It was at a church service in Munich that I saw him, a former S.S. man who had stood guard at the shower room door in the processing center at Ravensbruck. He was the first of our actual jailers that I had seen since that time. And suddenly it was all there – the roomful of mocking men, the heaps of clothing, Betsie's pain-blanched face.

He came up to me as the church was emptying, beaming and bowing. "How grateful I am for your message, Fraulein." He said. "To think that, as you say, He has washed my sins away!" His hand was thrust out to shake mine. And I, who had preached so often to the people in Bloemendaal the need to forgive, kept my hand at my side.

Even as the angry, vengeful thoughts boiled through me, I saw the sin of them. Jesus Christ had died for this man; was I going to ask for more? Lord Jesus, I prayed, forgive me and help me to forgive him. I tried to smile, I struggles to raise my hand. I could not. I felt nothing, not the slightest spark of warmth or charity. And so again I breathed a silent prayer. Jesus, I prayed, I cannot forgive him. Give me Your forgiveness.

As I took his hand the most incredible thing happened. From my shoulder along my arm and through my hand a current seemed to pass from me to him, while into my heart sprang a love for this stranger that almost overwhelmed me. And so I discovered that it is not on our forgiveness any more than on our goodness that the world's healing hinges, but on His. When He tells us to love our enemies, He gives, along with the command, the love itself."

—*The Hiding Place*

 PAUSE FOR THOUGHT …

Who do you need to forgive?

Notes

GROUP DISCUSSION

💬 What "power" did the young man in the video seem to be holding on to by withholding forgiveness? How do you think this will eventually come back to haunt him?

💬 Why does it seem easier to forgive someone who apologizes versus the person who refuses to acknowledge that he or she did anything wrong?

💬 What is the primary difference between forgiveness and reconciliation?

💬 Why do you think it's important to identify and assign value to the losses someone has created in your life before you can move toward forgiving him or her?

💬 How can an unwillingness to move toward forgiveness affect our relationship with God?

💬 In what sense can our spiritual health be measured by the health of our relationships (even with those with whom we are in conflict)?

💬 Under what circumstances can "asking for forgiveness" actually be manipulative? What needs to happen to prevent that question from being abused?

💬 In what sense does forgiveness mean transferring a debt that someone has created in your life to "God's repayment plan"? What options does your offender have to address that debt—once it only exists between him and God?

💬 How does believing that God will have the final word in all matters of injustice make it easier for us to move toward forgiving someone who has hurt us—especially those who remain remorseless?

💬 Does forgiving someone necessarily mean that you must trust that person again? Explain.

GROUP DISCUSSION

💬 Give some examples of where genuine forgiveness has taken place, but trust is wisely kept at a minimum.

💬 Give some examples of where it would be appropriate to *increase* your willingness to trust someone on the basis of his or her penitent words & actions.

💬 What does rebuilding trust look like? What's required for that to happen?

💬 How do you know when you've forgiven someone?

💬 Is there someone in your life whom you need to forgive? If so, where are you in that process? What do you need to do to move forward?

DAY ONE
NEGLECT
....

Now in these days when the disciples were increasing in number, a complaint by the Hellenists arose against the Hebrews because their widows were being neglected in the daily distribution. (Acts 6:1)

1. What was the complaint that the Hellenists had against the Hebrews?

2. Why do you think the Hellenist widows were being neglected?

3. What dark motives might the Hellenists be attributing to the Hebrews?

4. Why is it common to assign selfish motives to people with whom we may be in conflict? What often drives that tendency?

DAY TWO
DELEGATION
....

And the twelve summoned the full number of the disciples and said, "It is not right that we should give up preaching the word of God to serve tables. ³ Therefore, brothers, pick out from among you seven men of good repute, full of the Spirit and of wisdom, whom we will appoint to this duty. ⁴ But we will devote ourselves to prayer and to the ministry of the word." (Acts 6:2-4)

1. How did the Apostles respond to the complaint?

2. Why did the Apostles see the need to delegate this responsibility to someone else?

3. What were the qualifications and characteristics of the people to be chosen who would address the problem?

4. If you were to delegate an important responsibility to someone, what characteristics would you want that person to have?

DAY THREE
QUALIFICATIONS

And what they said pleased the whole gathering, and they chose Stephen, a man full of faith and of the Holy Spirit, and Philip, and Prochorus, and Nicanor, and Timon, and Parmenas, and Nicolaus, a proselyte of Antioch. [6] These they set before the apostles, and they prayed and laid their hands on them. (Acts 6:5-6)

1. How did everyone seem to express their enthusiasm for the Apostles' solution?

2. Who did they end up choosing for the task? What can we assume about these men?

3. How did the Apostles clearly communicate that they were delegating their authority to these seven men who were chosen for this task?

4. As reflected in the dispute between the Hellenists and the Hebrews, what are the characteristics of an effective biblical resolution to conflict?

DAY FOUR
RESULTS
....

And the word of God continued to increase, and the number of the disciples multiplied greatly in Jerusalem, and a great many of the priests became obedient to the faith. (Acts 6:7)

1. How did the resolution to this problem prove to be effective?

2. What happens in the Kingdom of God when conflict is addressed well and resolved?

3. What kind of simmering conflicts might be preventing growth in your circle of influence?

4. How can you effectively address those challenges?

OVERCOME EVIL WITH GOOD

*If the person with whom you
are in conflict is not willing to go
through these steps, be sure to stay
the course yourself.*

SESSION 8
OVERCOME EVIL WITH GOOD

▶ **PLAY VIDEO**

IN THE PREVIOUS SESSIONS...

- Where conflict comes from (Spark/Gasoline/Fire)

- We often want things too much (desires become demands), and so we fight and quarrel (James 4).

- The Slippery Slope—our natural tendencies to escape and attack

- The Gospel: It changes everything!

- The First G: Go to Higher Ground / Glorify God

  ▸ What would please and honor God in this situation?

- The Second G: Get Real About Yourself / Get the Log Out of Your Eye

  ▸ Start with your own contribution to a conflict

  ▸ Rooting out idols (going beyond the superficial and getting to the heart)

  ▸ A good confession (The 7 A's)

- The Third G: Gently Engage Others / Gently Restore

  ▸ Go talk to them (privately); Get help

- The Fourth G: Get Together on Lasting Solutions / Go and Be Reconciled

  ▸ Giving and receiving of forgiveness

  ▸ Heart vs. Transactional forgiveness

  ▸ The Four Promises of Forgiveness

OVERCOME EVIL WITH GOOD

So, I did everything and it didn't work. What do I do now?

> *"Do not be overcome by evil, but overcome evil with good. "*
> *Romans 12:21*

It Doesn't Completely Depend on You

Sometimes we strive for peace without "success." We do all the things that God calls us to, but our opponent continues to treat us unkindly, angrily, unfairly, or harshly.

Scripture makes it clear that it truly takes two to make peace. Romans 12:18 says, "If it is possible, **as far as it depends on you**, live at peace with everyone." It depends on the other person also, and sometimes they may not be ready or willing to do the right thing. And they may never get there.

Does success mean reconciliation? Not necessarily. Success may just be faithfulness, obedience, and keeping on doing the right thing.

The Big Temptation: Taking matters into your own hands

"God's way didn't work ... it must be time to try a new approach."

This approach inevitably leads us back to escaping or attacking (the very sinful responses from which we've worked so hard to be free).

God never wants us to "close our Bible" on any problem and fight the world's way. Second Corinthians 10:3-4 says, "For though we live in the world, we do not wage war as the world does. The weapons we fight with are not the weapons of the world." This means that we are to wage war (a spiritual war), but we are not to use the world's weapons. Instead, we are to use the spiritual weapons God gives us.

So, how do we proceed? Scripture provides valuable advice:

1) PRAY

> *"But I tell you: Love your enemies and pray for those who persecute you." Matt. 5:44*

Scripture makes it clear that God grants the gift of repentance (see 2 Timothy 2:25). Pray for your enemy's heart: only God can change it.

Remember to recognize your own limits:

Your Job: To honor God by doing the right thing

God's Job: To change people

2) GUARD YOUR HEART

"Bless those who persecute you, bless and do not curse." Rom. 12:14

Our temptation is to "curse" those who mistreat us. Remember "heart forgiveness" was a disposition to love your enemy even before you are reconciled. When you "bless and do not curse," you strive to maintain this heart disposition.

As we leave it with God, it leaves the door open for reconciliation, and is a constant protection for you against bitterness.

3) STAY CLOSE TO GODLY COUNSEL

"He who walks with the wise grows wise but a companion of fools suffers harm." Prov. 13:20

All Christians are surrounded by worldly advice, telling us to fight back, stand up for our rights, or take them to court. It is tempting to seek out this advice in times of conflict. (It is often seen in difficult marriages heading towards divorce.)

Seek out those people who will give you the advice you need to hear (not just what you want to hear), encouraging you to stay the course, endure under trial, and prioritize obeying God over all else.

4) KEEP ON DOING WHAT IS RIGHT

"Do not repay anyone evil for evil. Be careful to do what is right in the eyes of everybody." Rom. 12:17

We will have opportunities to attack our opponents in many different ways. David twice had the opportunity to kill Saul when Saul was pursuing him, but he would not "lift his hand against God's anointed" (see 1 Sam. 24:1-7; 26:5-11). We keep on doing what is right to try to win over our opponent and to obey God, who calls us to love our enemies.

5) THE ULTIMATE WEAPON: DELIBERATE FOCUSED LOVE

"On the contrary: 'If your enemy is hungry, feed him; if he is thirsty, give him something to drink. In doing this, you will heap burning coals on his head.' Do not be overcome by evil, but overcome evil with good." Rom. 12:20-21

We can use the same weapon God used to win us over: love.

Here we simply do something the world cannot understand and would never consider. We *love* our enemy. If he is hungry … if he is thirsty … We seek to meet our enemy's real-life, day-to-day needs.

We don't just resist evil with good, we can *overcome* evil with good. Unexpected, undeserved love can break down even the most stubborn heart.

FULL CIRCLE: IT ALL COMES BACK TO THE GOSPEL

At this moment our story ends where it began.

How can I keep on loving, praying for, and caring for someone who continues to mistreat me? I can, because that is exactly what Jesus did for me.

Jesus suffered more there than we will ever suffer. We can endure all things because of the gospel.

Closing Thought

When I see Jesus, "who as a sheep before its shearers is silent" (Isa. 53:7), taking my punishment without fighting back, I find the source of the power I need to lay down my "rights" and love beyond hope or reason to the amazement of a watching world.

The gospel ultimately changes our perspective on conflict.

GROUP DISCUSSION

💬 How do you know when you've fully obeyed Paul's command, *"If at all possible, as far as it depends on you, be at peace with all men."? (Romans 12:18)*

If you need some help answering this question, here's a checklist …

💬 1. On a scale of 1-to-10, how much do you want what the Lord wants—namely peaceful, flourishing relationships that honor God and the people involved?

💬 2. On a scale of 1-to-10, how much do you want a peaceful, flourishing relationship, if at all possible, with the person with whom you are in conflict?

💬 3. Have you identified your legitimate interests? Do you know the other person's legitimate interests? Would you be able to paraphrase those interests in a way that the other person would say, "Yes, you get it" ?

💬 4. Has there been any sinful expression or protection of legitimate interests in this conflict, either from you or the other person? If you're guilty of this, have you owned up to the dishonoring nature of your words and actions, and acknowledged full responsibility for impact it had on the people involved?

💬 5. In this, have you *modeled* for the other person the acknowledgement you would like to see from him or her in this conflict? Have you graciously described the impact of the other person's unhealthy words and actions upon you? What was that person's response?

💬 6. Are you moving toward forgiving the other person who has sinned against you in this conflict and created losses in your life (of any size or magnitude?) Have you identified, valued, and fully grieved those losses?

💬 7. Have you considered multiple solutions that address the legitimate interests of everyone involved?

💬 8. Have you made a wise decision in regard to increasing or decreasing your vulnerability to this person, based on his or her willingness to follow these steps? How would you describe the healthiest *level of reconciliation* with this person?

💬 9. When you give an account to God about the circumstances surrounding this conflict, will He say to you something along the lines of … "I was pleased with the way you handled that situation" … ?

If you can answer "yes" to questions 3-10, then you have fully followed the biblical command … *"If possible, so far as it depends on you, live peaceably with all."* (Romans 12:18)

If you're stuck at any of the steps above, seek godly counsel on how to remove the obstacles that may be hindering your progress.

We are here to help.

PEACEMAKER
MINISTRIES

On Your Own

Here are four days of Bible studies that you can do on your own that will take you a little deeper into the nature of conflict ...These passages highlight biblical ways to set limits with people who refuse to repent (while always keeping the door open for reconciliation).

DAY ONE
NOT WILLING

"O Jerusalem, Jerusalem, the city that kills the prophets and stones those who are sent to it! How often would I have gathered your children together as a hen gathers her brood under her wings, and you were not willing! [35] *Behold, your house is forsaken. And I tell you, you will not see me until you say, 'Blessed is he who comes in the name of the Lord!'"* (Luke 13:34-35)

1. What past destructive behaviors of Jerusalem's inhabitants did Jesus identify?

2. What was Jesus lamenting here? What did He want more than anything?

3. What was preventing Jesus from having a peaceful and flourishing relationship with most of the people in Jerusalem?

4. Why is important to respect a person's decision not to be reconciled with you?

DAY TWO
TWICE WARNED

As for a person who stirs up division, after warning him once and then twice, have nothing more to do with him, [11] knowing that such a person is warped and sinful; he is self-condemned. (Titus 3:10-11)

1. What type of person was Paul describing here? How can a pattern of divisive behavior (from one person) be so damaging to a church?

2. How many reasonable attempts are we to make with someone who is remorselessly divisive? What assumptions can we make about that person if he or she refuses to stop the damaging behaviors?

3. Why do you think God sets a limit on dealing with extraordinarily difficult people? Does that necessarily mean that you're closing the door forever on that relationship? If not, explain.

4. What would have to happen for you to make yourself vulnerable to such a person again?

DAY **THREE**
PAUL AND BARNABAS SEPARATE

And after some days Paul said to Barnabas, "Let us return and visit the brothers in every city where we proclaimed the word of the Lord, and see how they are." [37] Now Barnabas wanted to take with them John called Mark. [38] But Paul thought best not to take with them one who had withdrawn from them in Pamphylia and had not gone with them to the work. [39] And there arose a sharp disagreement, so that they separated from each other. Barnabas took Mark with him and sailed away to Cyprus, [40] but Paul chose Silas and departed, having been commended by the brothers to the grace of the Lord. [41] And he went through Syria and Cilicia, strengthening the churches. (Acts 15:36-41)

1. What did Paul want to team up with Barnabas to do?

2. Who did Barnabas want to bring? Why did Paul object?

3. Why do you think they were not able to resolve the issue? What could have happened to change the situation?

4. At what point is it reasonable and healthy to "part ways" with someone? What needs to happen (on your end) before that is even considered?

DAY FOUR
PAUL AND BARNABAS RECONCILE

These passages were written sometime after the conflict between Barnabas and Paul.

Or is it only Barnabas and I who have no right to refrain from working for a living?
(1 Corinthians 9:6)

1. What indication do we have here that Paul and Barnabas were able to reconcile their differences?

2. How do you imagine that happened?

Aristarchus my fellow prisoner greets you, and Mark the cousin of Barnabas (concerning whom you have received instructions—if he comes to you, welcome him. (Colossians 4:10)

Luke alone is with me. Get Mark and bring him with you, for he is very useful to me for ministry. (2 Timothy 4:11)

3. How did Paul's feelings about Mark change (according to these passages)? What do you think happened?

4. What are some creative ways to affirm people after we've resolved our conflicts with them? What long-lasting benefits usually come from being deliberate about doing this?

NEXT STEPS...
Where do you go from here?

"But be doers of the word, and not hearers only, deceiving yourselves."
James 1:22

Thank you so much for being a part of this group studying Resolving Everyday Conflict. We trust that you found it a valuable use of your time, and that, in addition to teaching helpful principles, it has changed your perspective on conflict in a way that will impact your life forever.

But we hope that this isn't the end.

Here are four specific steps you can take to maximize the impact of your investment:

1. Keep applying what you learned.

A few simple ways to do that:

■ Pull this study guide out periodically and review it.

■ Complete all the "On Your Own" sections and any of the discussion questions your group was not able to finish.

■ List a couple of the areas discussed in this study that you would like to improve in your own life. Then share those areas with a trusted friend who can pray for you—and check in on you occasionally.

■ If God has been working on your heart regarding a certain relationship that is broken, don't just let that drop. Reach out to that person and apply the principles from this study to seek true and full reconciliation.

Get help if you need it. Remember, reconciliation is close to God's heart!

2. Study peacemaking in other ways.

Peacemaker Ministries has many other materials that will help you learn and grow in the area of peacemaking. You can discover more of these at www.peacemaker.net.

3. Teach the principles to others.

The best way to make sure you understand the material is to teach it to someone else. Here are a few simple ways:

Invite one or two friends out for coffee or lunch and walk them through the basic principles of peacemaking (as summarized in this guide), or volunteer to lead another group through this study in your church, neighborhood, or workplace.

4. Get to know Peacemaker Ministries better.

Again, Peacemaker Ministries is here to walk beside you as you deepen your understanding of biblical peacemaking. For instance, you can:

■ Visit www.peacemaker.net and look at all the free online resources that are available. While you are there, subscribe to PeaceMeal (a weekly e-devotional) and Reconciled (the Peacemaker Ministries newsletter).

■ Pursue more formal training in peacemaking (e.g., Conflict Coaching / Mediation or Certification as a Christian conciliator). This training would be particularly helpful if you frequently find yourself helping others to resolve their conflicts.

■ Attend a Peacemaker Conference. This conference happens every year in the fall; if you want to gather with like-minded people, come to a Peacemaker Conference! See www.peacemakerconference.net for details. Be sure to sign up for the Peacemaker Seminar if you haven't attended one yet.

■ Become a financial partner. Peacemaker Ministries is largely funded by donations from its financial partners. You may not be in a position to give right now, and that's OK. But if you've read this far, you obviously have an interest in the ministry of reconciliation, and we want to be up-front about the need. See www.peacemaker.net/donate for details.

Again, thank you for your commitment to this study and to the principles you've learned. May God richly bless you as you continue to seek to respond to everyday conflict in a radically different way.

TRAINING IN PEACEMAKING

Are you interested in helping others work through their conflicts? Has God given you a passion to dig deeper as a peacemaker?

If so, we invite you to go through further training with Peacemaker Ministries.

Peacemaker Ministries' training is designed to supplement and build upon the basic principles of peacemaking given to us in Scripture. There are two basic levels of training available: Foundational Skills and Advanced Training. This training is an integral part of embedding peace into your church, your vocation, and every aspect of life.

Foundational Skills Training

This level of training provides the tools you will need to effectively help people with most conflicts. The core of this training is the Conflict Coaching and Mediation event, four days of live instruction that will provide you with the opportunity to observe, practice, and discuss the process of biblical peacemaking.

Advanced Training

This training builds upon the skills acquired in the Foundational Skills Training while increasing your ability to assist others involved in more complex and difficult conflicts (such as marriage and divorce, multiple parties/multiple issues, formal arbitration and reconciling church conflict). Through these advanced courses, you will also have the opportunity to apply to our Certification Program, if you want to work toward the distinction of Certified Christian Conciliator™.

For more information or to find training near you, visit www.peacemaker.net/path-of-a-peacemaker/

TM

PEACEMAKER CONFERENCE

Each fall, people from around the globe with an interest in peacemaking gather at our Peacemaker Conference. Over the span of a few days, they enjoy notable plenary speakers, attend workshops, worship, relax, and experience deep fellowship with others who are of the same mind and heart. Bringing a group from your church or organization to the conference is a great way to gain a common vision for peacemaking.

For more information, see www.peacemakerconference.net

Keep up-to-date with the latest in peacemaking by signing up for *free* publications (print and electronic) available at www.peacemaker.net!